A Novel By
Susan Walcott

THE POSSESSED

For Shade, Seth and Eric

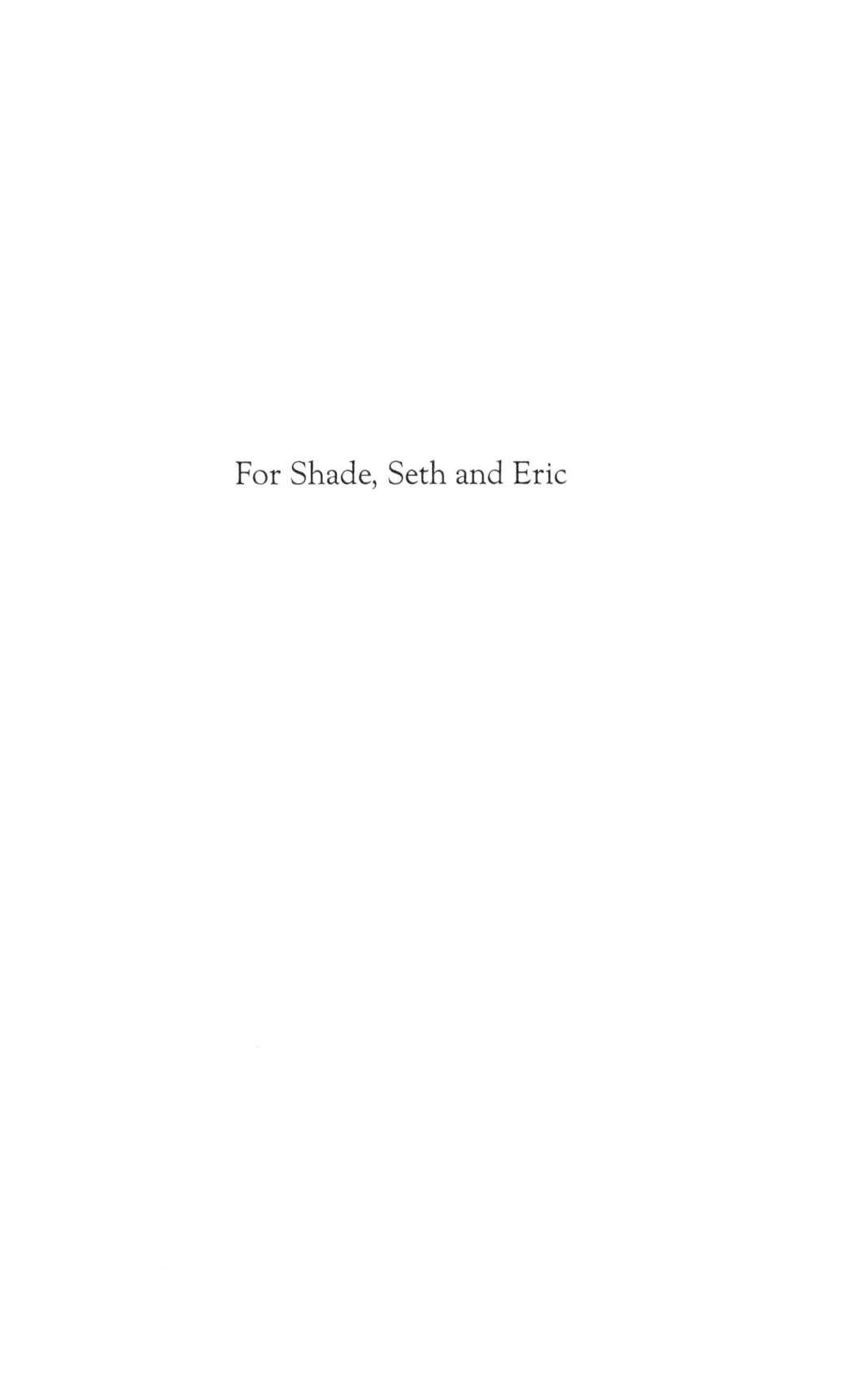

A3D Impressions

The Possessed
Susan Walcott

A3D Impressions
Tucson | Minneapolis

Copyright © 2024 Susan Walcott

All rights reserved, including the right to reproduce this book or portions thereof in any form whatsoever. Contact A3D Impressions Rights & Permission, a3dimpressions@gmail.com
awareness3d.com

This book is a work of fiction. Names, characters, places, and incidents either are products of the author's imagination or are used fictitiously. Any resemblance to actual events or locales or persons, living or dead, is entirely coincidental.

First A3D Impressions Edition November 2024

Publisher's Cataloging-in-Publication data

Names: Walcott, Susan, author.
Title: The possessed / Susan Walcott.
Description: Tucson, AZ; Minneapolis, MN: A3D Impressions, An impression of Awareness3D, LLC, 2024
Identifiers: LCCN: 2024915396 | ISBN: 979-8-9905270-0-3
Subjects: LCSH Counterculture--United States--History--20th century--Fiction. | Cults--Fiction. | Jesus People--Fiction. | Veterans--Fiction. | Coming of age--Fiction. | BISAC FICTION / Historical / 20th Century / General | FICTION / General
Classification: LCC PS3623. A53 P67 2024 | DDC 813.6--dc23

ISBN 979-8-9905270-0-3
LCCN: 2024915396

Acknowlegements

Kevin Lee Lopez, Dakota Sioux, acted as my editor, giving last minute help in my idiosyncratic punctuation. Even more than this help in editing, in the years I have known Kevin, he has shared the traditions, language, stories, songs, and ceremonies of his tribe.

The Lakota ceremonies grounded me. Learning to sing in the lodge gave me a voice. Understanding the language changed the way I experience nature and the world around me. And the use of tobacco gave me a connection to that world we call Makah.

Lakota language translations

Aho: Sacred 'Yes' or acknowledgment.
Canli: Tobacco (considered the most precious gift from Creator to the two leggeds)
Canunpa: Sacred Pipe
Hanwi: Moon (Wi's companion)
Inipi: Sweat Lodge
Inyan: Stone people
Makah: Mother Earth
Mitakuyas: shortened version of Mitakuye Oyasin: All my relations.
Mni Wakan Olowan: Sacred Water Song
Omakiyayo: Help me
Oyate: People or Nation
Pilamiyayelo: Thank you in men's language. Woman nation would say Pilamiya.
Sunka Wakan: Sacred dog literally, meaning Horse. (Lakota people thought they were looking at a sacred dog the first time they encountered horses).
Tatanka: Buffalo
Tunkasila: Grandfather
Unci Makah: Grandmother Earth
Wakan: Sacred
Wakan Tanka: Sacred Mystery
Wanagi: Ghost or spirit
Wasichu: Eaters of the fat. Often but not always referring to white people who historically took the best for themselves.
Wi: Sun
Wopila: A sacred thanks, often expressed as a give away

PART I

THE POSSESSED

Wade

❖

Too early waking, crawling around in darkness, damp tent, feeling for damp clothes cold stiff boots, rush out into the rain, into the mudsucking. Overhead, underfoot more mud thanGod nowhere in camp that isn't mildewed and damp.

The wood chip trail leads from tent street through fir trees past an outhouse to the dining hall where the brethren line up. Long haired, bearded men in flannel and denim or army surplus fatigues; sisters in long skirts over long-johns or Levi's silent wait. The line this morning, every morning, is slow, the wait long. The brethren are impatient to eat, they watch the serving window where the sisters dish out food, hoping for something filling, something sweet. The craving for sugar gnaws and they secretly bring in ice cream when allowed to visit town. I secretly bring in ice cream.

This morning it's cornmeal mush, yogurt made from our goats' milk and honey from our bee hives spread out against the woods on the edge of the pasture. Brother from Montana, hooded, mitted and veiled, worked the hives last summer for honey now in these dark days of winter.

Charlie sets his food down on the long table lowers his head, prays over his breakfast.

"Thirty-eight straight days of rain so far, think it's a record?" Charlie asks.

"No, not for here, they say sometimes it starts raining like this in August, July sometimes even. Short summers, no fall, late spring. You're in for it now, ha. Think you'll still be here this time next year?"

"Lord willing. But I might get sent out to one of the houses, there's a new house opening up in Savannah, Georgia, might get sent there. Learn all about southern hospitality, southern peaches, southern belles. Hmm.

"Shut up Charlie."

"Just saying."

"I mean it."

Charlie slides away cowers over his plate, turns to Andrew on his right but Andrew doesn't talk, just prays, so Charlie works on his mush. Charlie with the longest beard here at Zion, Charlie whose long lanky body is more skeleton than flesh. Uriah Heep, walking out of the pages David Copperfield. As long as I've known him I can't get that image out of my head - and always he's skulking around the kitchen and coming to work with extra biscuits in his pockets. He leaves the table then goes back up to the window to beg for more.

"You and me are moving that pig barn today." Charlie says, coming back with a second bowl of mush.

"I kinda don't think it's actually even possible to walk that thing across the pasture. Who's idea was it to use it for an infirmary?" Charlie shakes his head.

"Liam had a dream about it. You complaining?"

"No, no, not me. Thing is we got all that lumber, why not just build it from scratch? And who's idea was it anyway to use that filthy building for the sister's infirmary?" Charlie shakes his head again, digs into his mush, mumbles under his breath.

"Liam had a dream and then the Lord spoke to him in a prophesy. We're supposed to be good stewards over what the Lord's already given us, plus we need it right away. With this flu taking over the camp we don't have the time to draw up plans and everything else it'd take to get it built. We need it now."

Charlie and I make our way outside, stand in the cold rain waiting, shuffling feet, breath like smoke, teeth chattering, moving back and forth trying to get the blood moving outside the warmth of the dining hall. At the edge of the pasture the fir trees glitter for a moment in the spearshaft of sunlight that breaks through and holds, then disappears. Nice gesture.

Paul, Captain of Tens, calls us together. Long, fervent prayer among the brethren then off to work at the edge of the pasture. Paul who lives for the spotlight. He stands off always keeping a distance but his prayers are constant. Not religious so much, just highly disciplined.

Lily

❖

Mouldering steam rises up from the shavings with each pitchfork. In the wheelbarrow is a mound of steaming manure. Vienna and Maggie, two paint mares, stand in the rain waiting to eat after their stalls are cleaned and refreshed with new straw. Tony, a tall bay thoroughbred gelding, is in a stall in back, he reaches his nose out through the little window above his feeder and drops hay onto the path leading out to the bee hives. Maggie is a youngster just under three years old, Vienna's offspring. Vienna is an older brood mare once again in foal, her belly the size of a small elephant trapped between narrow shoulders and hips. She'a a good patient horse, trots in circles teaching the elders, Liam and the others, to sit or post to the trot and canter so that when Armageddon begins and the world is breaking up we will be able to get around on horses.

I pass through the stall door, aim for the little wagon, run the wheelbarrow up the short ramp, dump the load and stop to catch my breath. In the short moment between loads I rub my hands together, try to thaw them but the damp cold burrows into the joints steadily as the morning slowly passes on.

From here I can see inside Liam and Cass's trailer. Cass is walking back and forth with an infant in her arms. It's warm inside the trailer and dry, this watching feels warm, feels secure. Living in a trailer with electricity, running water and toilets, a heater, a refrigerator with fruit with milk. Thoughts are sin, I know better but I can't help it. Cass drinks tea and sings lullabies and watches me work with the horses. Watches the men wrestle against boards, creating paths in the mud. There's a reason behind all this struggle, Liam says, it's all about trusting God. It's about learning the voice of God. It's about meeting God head on and living to tell the tale. We can't know this unless we're tested against ourselves and finally come to our limit. Then God is visible. At the end of this icy rain and mud God is visible.

Sawyer

❖

The brothers gather in the pasture at the edge of the forest, form a circle, long, fervent prayer among the brethren. Then wait in silence for Liam to get us started. From the forest the sound of breaking branches and hoofbeats breaks the silence; the heavy hoof beat, the long irregular rhythm, clunky, awkward, clearly elk.

Within the shadow of firs away from the voices of the brothers the herd takes visible shape in the minds eye. Marty beside me listens in serious silence.

"You know what it would mean to bring in an elk for the brethren?" I ask.

Marty nods.

We both listen to the fading sound of hoofbeats.

"If you're coming then come on, whatever it is, they're movin' fast."

We follow the distant sound of breaking branches up a long narrow trail trying for quiet, pacing our footsteps at uneven intervals to mask the too easily recognizable sound of human footfalls. Once on BLM land, the forest becomes darker, denser from decades of growth without human interference. Douglas firs spire upward in the dim morning light, spans of spider webs, illuminated by droplets of rain and mist zigzag from branch to branch catching us across the face and throat. Short stunted firs, spindly and uneven press against the dark and overcast sky, seeking nourishment from a light that is not available. Bracken ferns, azaleas and blackberry brambles cover the forest floor between long fallen logs. Marty's mouth goes dry, he has never been outside the confines of a manicured park and shudders at the chaos.

The sight of newly disturbed black earth angling up a steep hill draws us in further. I squat down, take up a handful of soft, moist, black earth, smell it, crush it.

"The tracks are too big for deer. I knew it. It's elk for sure," I whisper. "A small herd, maybe five, four for sure."

Steam rises from a massive pile of manure, fresh and warm along the trail. I know hunting and I know my scent is a dead give away. I dig into the manure barehanded, smear my jacket and pants, then spread it over my hands and face. When I motion to Marty to put some on my back, turning, waiting, Marty hesitates too long so I dig in and quickly rub manure on Marty's jacket then lie on my back and roll like a dog.

The hunt requires focus, never wavering focus as we continue up the trail. All instincts are heightened as we plunge into the ancient, ancestral memory of predator and prey. A quick backward glance is all that's needed to silence Marty and in that moment Marty signals, silently motions with his face to look. A group of four elk are just coming visible on the ridge not more than thirty feet away. A large bull among them and one calf. Without a sound I pull an old hunting knife from a leather sheath beneath my parka. My absolute focus is on the bull. Silently off the path, obscured by undergrowth, I circle to a position parallel the herd and slowly move in. The small herd continues eating but the bull flicks one ear, blasts out a deafening snort and the whole herd bolts up the trail.

Scrambling up the trail, off the trail, brambles and branches fly past. I see only broken earth, follow churned up earth, feel only the surge of adrenaline, the sweet reward of the hunt.

In the far distance the sound settles, the herd moves quietly now, a cautious stealth yet quicker than I can manage quietly. The trail is unmistakable though, chewed up from the elk. Toward the top of a ridge, well into BLM land and close on to the Cascade range, the tracks disappear at an outcropping of large boulders.

From this height the view of the Cascades stretches out forever; the endless rise and fall of mountain and valley fading into the distance. The elk are nowhere. Disturbed earth and broken branches visible about three hundred feet below mark where the elk reentered the dense forest. I stop, wait for Marty and to catch my breath.

The trail is easy to follow but for Marty, a challenge. A wide open path runs straight up the steepest part of the mountain. The final climb, a short stretch over boulders and twigs, takes Marty an extra half hour. The mist and rain we walked through early on and that has soaked us down in Zion everyday for the past month is now below us and from this plateau the sun shines through, strong and clear. The carpet of firs above the mist to the South sparkles. To the West valleys and ridges glow like a sequined cloth folded in upon itself, like diamonds brilliant and shimmering. Marty pauses, looks heavenward and proclaims his fealty to the Lord of Hosts. Below in the valley clouds cling like a lake. Up here our little plateau is an island above the clouds. In this sun I rest like I haven't for a long time, spread eagle against a warm boulder taking in the heat of the sun.

"Come join me," I say.

"I thought you'd be down following the herd."

"Nah, I want to give 'em a chance to relax a bit. They'll slow back down, return to grazing if they think we've stopped tracking 'em. Celebrate the sun a moment, it might be the last we see of it for many months."

"You want me to go back, get the gun, let them know what we're doing?"

"No, we're too far up now. It'd take you all the rest of the morning and by then they'd be long gone. No, it's just you and me . . . . It's the Lord's gift." Below, in the valley, the sound of breaking branches and then the bull bellows again. We both look down the trail.

"He wouldn't a brought us these elk if He didn't want us to hunt 'em, provide nourishment for the people. If we can bring back one, the women can scrape the hide and we'll have leather too. It was the Lord led us, sure as I'm standing here."

Below, out from under the canopy, the huge bull elk comes into view with his massive antlers. Marty can't take his eyes off the huge animal.

"Breathe, brother. And stay put."

Easing silently toward the elk, over the granite boulders, the long slow hike down to the trail and the herd, gaining ground till I'm close enough to smell them, hear their breathing, the crunch of their chewing. I angle my body away from the herd, slip my knife out of its sheath, slouch in a submissive posture. The bull looks over at me, sees no threat, snorts and continues eating, satisfied there is no danger. In this way I close the distance to three yards, two yards. With the suddenness of a bolt, lunging at the nearest cow, I catch her in the throat with the knife. Bleeding out but still alive she runs with the herd up the side of the mountain, through brush, over downed trees until they all disappear over the ridge.

Charlie

❖

Paul, Captain of Tens, calls us to prayer, shoulder to shoulder, in a tight knit circle. Long, fervent prayers make their way around as each of the brothers speaks his heart. Somehow he's capable of getting our attention without trying, some unconscious knee jerk reaction on our part is my guess. Plus he's aloof, holds himself back from friendships, keeps his own council out here even though we're supposed to be brethren, brothers in Christ.

"There it is," Paul says to no one in particular, pointing to the small twelve by ten foot wood framed building at the farthest end of the pasture up against the woods.

Last summer I watched a mother pig give birth to eight babies then pant in the sweltering heat nursing them all summer long. The misery of it stuck with me and I never went out to the pig barn after that. Then the Lord moved in Liam's heart and told him to get rid of the pigs for the sake of the Children of Israel who were not allowed to eat pork.

"We're moving it to the near side of the horse barn by the

dog pens," Paul says. "Sisters will clean it out then we'll have an infirmary for them. Praise the Lord. With all the sickness we've had this past month really we need it."

I look back at the tool shed. Wood-stove fire burning hot, all steamy inside, smoke rising from the pipe. I should try to get that stewardship. Check tools out, let the wet workers clean their own mudstuck shovels while I count tools and stuff.

"Be a vessel of the Lord," Paul says, looking into the near distance, staring out across the pasture at the pig barn in that actor-in-a-role kinda way he has. Repeating what we hear Liam say everyday, but making it sound like he's the first to ever say it.

The plan is roll it across the pasture then through another 600 feet of mud on logs we took from the forest. "Be a vessel of the Lord," I say to myself, shaking my head in disbelief. Paul looks toward the woods waiting for Liam. It's on his watch that the two men disappeared into the woods. Too quick to do anything, too sudden to realize they weren't coming back and now he has to speak for them.

The brothers start work moving logs out of the woods, wanting to get to work, easier in this icy chill to be working than standing. To the side of the dirt road just inside the woods are logs stacked six high. Two to a log, the men carry them to the pasture near the shed, back and forth until there are ten. Liam joins us, a Prophet of God, standing taller than any one of us. Around his head swirls a halo, his white hair and beard stand out from his ruddy, gaunt features and lately his pale blue eyes have taken on a wild intensity that I've only seen before in fellow speed freaks. He steps toward the men coming out of the woods carrying logs.

"Move those logs to the front of the shed and wait for the others before you try to lift. We need more logs, there are supposed to be more men here. What about Sawyer and Marty? Aren't they supposed to be here? Did anyone see them this morning?"

One of the men holding a log says he saw them run off into the woods after hearing hoofbeats, hasn't seen them since. Paul speaks up repeats that he saw Sawyer run off into the woods as well, Marty followed.

"Well if they're not back in the next half hour they can pack up their things. We are vessels of the Holy Spirit who has called us here and not our own. We don't decide if it's a good day for us to yield to God's voice or not. Our commitment is to the Holy Spirit and when we start running after the flesh or hoofbeats, hoofbeats! Unbelievable. If the Lord calls on you to drop everything and travel to another state to evangelize and set up a new house, then you better well start packing. No questions asked, 'be instant in season and out of season.' That's how we walk with God. Not second guessing hoofbeats." Liam's voice breaks and jabs, rises in plaintive emphasis. Some New York twist to it makes you feel guilty about something unnamed.

"Wade, you go, see if you can find those two but don't be long. Charlie you go with him."

Darkness under the forest canopy and cloud cover, we stop a minute, let our eyes adjust, listen in silence. Wade struts on ahead, lets out a long sigh and pushes the hood back off his head and away from his clean shaven face, his slicked back hair. Out here in the mud he tries so hard to be clean, sneaks into the laundry room to iron his bluejeans, impossible task but it keeps him going, thinking he's someday going to be a leader, his head held high, eyes glistening in childlike wonder with the task at hand and with the fact that Liam called him out by name.

Moving slow and quiet through dew drenched spider webs, a primeval world, breathe in the forest, pine needles underfoot, soft moldering earth, sweet honeyed fragrance of blackberry brambles, trees growing in darkness, darkness in their bones and in their bloodsap. So much black earth, abundant, fertile, fecund, rich. These woods thrive in a darkness I can taste. Feels like I'm on acid.

"What are you doing?"

Wade's voice snaps like a shockwave against my chest, a knocking brittleness and I flinch, stand up quickly against his authority clutching handfuls of earth and decomposing leaves, watching the forest vibrate in fading waves of color . . . "Keep moving, what are you looking at me for?"

Another hundred yards up the trail we stop, listen, there is no sound except our own breathing, no footfalls or breaking twigs. Ears adjust to quiet like eyes adjust to darkness and now as the soft breeze passes through, the needles sound a single high pitched note and the voices of the men waiting at the edge of the pasture drift in through the trees and mingle with the sound of rain dripping off branches but no Sawyer and no Marty.

Sawyer, questionable Sawyer. Threw a plate of butter back at the sisters through the dining hall window into the kitchen because it was hard, shouting they couldn't even thaw butter, stupid women. Hmm, just as well if he gets kicked out. Not Marty though, he's a child still. A babe in the Lord, an innocent lamb.

"Maybe they circled back left the woods for the dining hall or something. Whatever, they aren't here now and I don't think we can stand to lose two more backs to the woods."

"You give up too easy, Wade. We haven't even gotten out of earshot of the brothers."

"We can follow those churned up tracks. If they're tracking something I'd have to guess that would be it. Starts just up there, off that deer trail. But we don't have to follow them to know what they're up to and where they're going. Sawyer wouldn't turn around for us anyway - just because we asked nicely," Wade calls back on his way back down the trail.

Lily

❖

"Make a fulcrum with these larger logs set down parallel to the sides and with these smaller ones pushed under to pry it up out of the mud," Liam calls out. More men come down from the dining hall and from the cabins and tents nestled in the trees. They make a circle around the building and tie ropes around, tying it up on the sides where they hammered boards down low so they could help lift it.

From beneath the cover of the horse barn the men look small, their jackets dark from the rain, but their pained faces are clear even from this distance. Liam points, "Place those logs there, sideways, and those over there, under. Same on each side. There's your fulcrum. Lift the front now and slide the roller logs under."

Together they lift as men in front press the logs down creating leverage against the logs running parallel to the sides until the front lifts. The mud is deep from the men trampling in the rain, it's been raining daily since early October and now it's late November.

"Slide those logs under, let her down easy, down easy on those logs. Now, roll the logs beneath, all five."

The men scramble to roll the logs in place as the shed lifts above the earth with a sucking sound. The earth no more wants to let it go than these men want it to, secretly hoping it would never have gotten this far. Their faces are solemn, serious. The weight of the building presses their boots deeper into the mud.

The rain slants into the horse barn, it's not misting anymore, it's a full on downpour. Mensounds mingle with the racket on the tin roof, sounds that cut and burn, sad awful groans from trying to do the impossible. "If you get enough strong backs," he said, and they believed it but then the sound of wood twisting back on itself, squealing and snapping, moving along the ground with the slaggy sound of mud. *'Verily, verily I say unto you whatsoever you ask in my name it shall be given to you.'*

Andrew

❖

And he made bars of Shit-tim wood; five for the boards of the one side of the tabernacle, and five bars for the boards of the other side of the tabernacle for the sides westward.

And he made the middle bar to shoot through the boards from the one end to the other. Exodus 36:31-3

Faces move about the dim, same to same, eyes in deep sockets, noses long, aquiline, short, broken. Glittering hair pasted to foreheads in the rain. Saints all, in the shadows beneath the everyday, under hoods, under hats, shadows shape faces. Saints and Martyrs, witnesses of the faith, temples of the Lord, cleansed by our works for the Lord. Shadrach, Meshach, Abednego stood before the fire, we stand in the face of endless rain but the Lord will not kill us again with rain. And so we carve God's promise out of wood; timber from the forest while the hand of God is upon us daily speaking through Liam.

Liam, a giant among us, a prophet of God, a second Moses

in the wilderness guiding the new Children of Israel, because we are building the promise land with our bare hands. The second generation is us and we come with fire in our hearts and tools in our hands because we will build a city apart. We are Saints all, vessels of the most high God.

"Those logs there, sideways, and one under toward the shed. Same on each side. There's your fulcrum. Be the tool of God, a fulcrum to the Lord."

As these logs bear the weight of the tabernacle you will bear the weight of the service of the Lord and as this mud cries out from beneath to draw down the building of the Saints, so will Satan, my enemy, try to draw you down. Therefore you must fight the temptation to sink into your sinfulness, the temptation of your flesh against the purity of my spirit in you. I alone know the thoughts of the heart and I alone know what you have in your heart, the lust, the cravings, the carnal thoughts. It is My will that you purify yourself in these woods that I have given you for your cleansing.

Thank you Lord, Praise you Lord.

"Andrew, yo, pay attention. Stand back over there." Under the poncho Liam's face like the others hidden in outlines but for the white hair, glowing. "I want you to push from behind once the shed is in place on the logs and ready to roll. Yes, there. Then you take the log as it comes out from behind and bring it around to the front and we'll put it under and keep this thing rolling. Move it toward the horse barn, in that direction. You men, clear that stuff out of the way, that equipment, when we get closer. Paul, stand back with Andrew, help him with those logs. You see what it is needs to move? Andrew, keep up there, catch the log soon as it comes out the back side run it to the front. Paul help him. Now we're rolling, keep it moving."

"Lily," Liam calls ahead, "this thing's gonna to go right by where that mare's standing. Lock both mares inside the stalls so they don't spook with this walking building."

Lily. That night from the door of my tent I saw you move like a feather floating across the surface of water, driven by wind, etching the surface. It is good that a man should leave the house of his father and mother and cleave to his wife and they two shall be one flesh. And let the wives look to their own husbands for everything. Everything. Everything, praise the Lord.

"Andrew, keep up there, pay attention to the work, catch the log soon as it comes out the back side. Run it to the front quickly so we don't lose the momentum."

Marty

❖

"She's dead, she just don't know it yet," Sawyer shouts back. I angle down the steep trail toward Sawyer and together we follow the tracks only now without the carefulness and silence of the hunt.

"I like this part, tracking without the pressure. Of course the tracks are easier to follow now she's thrashing about. She's a good one, a beauty. I could smell the blood, hit the jugular for sure. She'll be close, no way she could travel far."

The tracks lead upward to the rocky heights without any sign of the young elk. We stop to survey the vast range in front of us. Mountains as far as the horizon, an unbroken expanse of firs blanketing the surface, hiding the surface, hiding the elk.

Sawyer squats on his haunches, pulls out a cigarette from within the lining of his jacket, lights up and takes a long, deep drag. "Don't look so shocked, Marty."

"It's just that we're not supposed to."

"God's not interested in us having a smoke out here on His mountain, trust me. Here," he says, passing me a cigarette.

"This is real," I say, finally, after lighting up. "Men on the mountain tracking elk. Enjoying a smoke."

"Don't say nothing about this," Sawyer says. "We'd get kicked out of the ministry for sure. We're only doing this because we need a moment to regroup. Regroup and figure out where that elk went. Now we can't see them with our eyes we use our ears, we use our noses. Close your eyes, Marty, tell me what you see."

I close my eyes, try to hear past the pulsing of blood in my ears, past the absence of olfactory nerves due to the smoke, try to tap into my as yet unknown prayer sense of God's voice speaking, telling me where she wandered off to. "I think they're over there," I say, pointing south.

"Why do you say that?"

"Don't know, just do."

The crack of a twig to the south and both of us strain in that direction, listening, watching for any movement within the tree cover. Sawyer rises without speaking and zigzags along the steep granite shelf, looking for signs of a trail or tracks leading into the woods below. The sun is past its zenith as we begin our descent into the western region of BLM territory. The tracks, just visible at the edge of the stone ridge, abruptly stop then start up again down below the ridge and head south.

Sawyer travels down the narrow trail quickly and surely, sidestepping boulders and branches, keeping an even pace without regard to my occasional falls. In the distance, a stream glistens, picking up sunlight that shafts randomly through the forest. The sun still shining through the thinning clouds is visible down below in the forest. Sawyer won't stop even though the shadows are growing longer. He, we, are of one mind in pursuit of the game.

Yet we haven't sighted the elk since dropping down onto this trail, haven't seen sign of the elk other than the first tracks leading from the top. The sound of water moving over rocks fills the air when we stop to listen.

"You think we're still on track?" I ask finally, hoping for another cigarette break.

"I do, the tracks are constant if light. I think they're either slowed way down or the cow I stuck is on her own. Either way we're still following her. Look here, this branch has a trace of fur, the same brown as them elk and look, yes, ha, yes, blood, right here, see here on these leaves? See? Alright, they're probably down at the creek. We need to move silent now as apparently I didn't catch the jugular like I thought."

Again with uneven steps we wind our way down cutbacks toward the creek.

"See here? The mushed up trail stops suddenly once they hit the backside of the mountain, like they suddenly stopped rushing and began to quiet and look for grazing again. Tracks all lead down, all except for this. Look here, this broken twig and a brushed and soiled fallen limb. That's where the one veered off and continued on her own and now we have a track to follow.

"Look on down that trail, Marty. You can see how it's disturbed and down that other one there. See it? See it? The one went that way, you better believe it and you better believe we'll find her down. Down and needing to be bled."

Tracks and the smell of blood. The smell of blood guides Sawyer. "I know she's on her own. I can smell blood at two hundred feet. Always been able to track by smell. And I'm right." Sawyer kneels and quiets to a whisper, "off there, you see her?"

I scramble toward the fallen elk, outrun Sawyer and stand over her like a hero or a marksman posing for a photo with my foot on her haunch.

"She looks to weigh around 1000 pounds good size for a cow maybe three seasons to her. Doesn't look like she's nursed. Might be carrying. I love the feel of elk, the gangling look. Not deer, not moose, something in between," Sawyer says.

"I didn't believe we'd find her," I say, taking my foot off, kneeling down to look closer then jumping back. "Oh, disgusting! she's crawling with ticks. How're we going to get her down with all these ticks?"

"Light her on fire that's how. But first we got to bleed her. She's warm still and we have to move quickly."

Sawyer's knife blade is sharp, slices her throat easy as butter.

Warm blood flows, not pumping just a steady release. Soft throat, white and new, new winter coat, soft, fresh.

"Hate to burn this beautiful coat off but these ticks'll move to us now there's no blood to be had on her.

"It'll take work to get even the smallest fire going. First thing is dig down under the dense areas under the trees where the rain might not have seeped. We need kindling and some twigs. The forest isn't going to be easy on us, she won't yield to us just because we're here. Once we get it going good the fur will char off and the ticks will burn off. Over there, we'll start that fire over there and then we'll have light and warmth and we can singe her with burning sticks. That's right just there near that downed log off the trail. Her heart and liver will sustain us tonight . . . ."

"Tonight?"

"Yeah, tonight. There's no way we can get all this done and hike her out tonight. It's getting dark fast in case you didn't notice. It'a pitch-black out here at night and the sky's got maybe an hour before that. Even if we started now we'd be in darkness before we reached the next ridge over, and from there I need to see to find us back. What'd you think? We're going to take the tram home? Ha, Marty, this is real now, figure it out. We'll start the fire and then go for more dry wood."

Julian

❖

Sewer drains send up mists, spirits take shape, come to life each night the sun sets and the sky darkens. Nights dense with spirits. I see them with my trained eyes, eyes trained to see enemies moving, only the slightest visible movement and I see it, sensitive to the visual; enemies, ghosts, and what held it together - my scope. Outside that small circle chaos reigned, inside my scope all was still all was silent all was clear. I knew who I was inside that circle searching the distances for enemy movement. And I know it will never be the same again I will never be the same again because at that moment there was only one way out and it was down. Nothing holds together here now the war's over, my war's over. The rain in Illyria is familiar but the smells are all wrong something missing some familiar smellsound gone awry. Once upon a time it all made sense. Once upon a time I was a boy waiting to be a man. Speak for myself think for myself suffer for my own mistakes but something interfered and now I stuttering confounded think wrong suffer wrong. Doesn't matter, doesn't matter throw it all away, myself, my life, nothing matters

I can't see right anymore too big a circle, too much crashing in.

Julian comes from the North, a land of endless plains and sacred mountains. A land surrounded by immovable, implacable, calcified discrimination. A land of Ancestors and Relatives. The latter living in old, run down reservation houses, waiting for the end of the centuries long winter. The former living in the recesses of the hills and the eddies of the streams; still and quiet yet always present, always waiting.

He carries himself proud and steely, a protective, evocative posture passed down on the rez from generation to generation. It is a learned carriage, an armor that his body has grown to fit. His long black hair is held back in two braids which drip rain onto his Levi's. A green bandana keeps stray hairs away from his young face. His old jacket is too thin to keep out the cold but it was a homecoming gift from his uncle when he returned from the war so he wears it for the inner warmth. He owns nothing and wants nothing.

These two years since returning from Nam, Julian has wandered the streets of Illyria; his response to a necessity that lives inside the body, holding him, keeping him in place until that necessity should show itself. But time drags slowly here. This staying in Illyria, this not knowing why weighs heavily. Nam reduced him. The order, the structure, the unsustainable hierarchy reduced him. He finds himself waiting for orders but there are no orders, no directions, no direction. He waits but the hollow air surrounds him with silence.

The street veers off toward the bright lights of downtown, Julian turns down a darkened alley toward the soft glow of a distant backlit window at the far end - his safe place in the city. That window, the soft flicker of a candle just visible behind a curtain, like a smell brings on the memory of place where carefree thoughts run freely and good music and laughter ring of innocence. Innocence. He is held there and separated, both, by the curtain and the memory and the pressure of something crushing in on his chest.

But there, leaning against the wall across from the very

window, in his spot, his spot! is Davis. The shock of seeing Davis throws him back to an earlier time, one not innocent, not free, and he squats behind a dumpster and waits; quiets his breathing, slows his pulse, on alert not ready to believe it is Davis. If he waits long enough this Davis will go away like all the other ghosts from his company who visit him. But this Davis is not going away.

The man steps away from the graffitied wall to face Julian, real flesh and blood Davis not his ghost. Wearing army issue pants and army issue hair, Davis' slim body seems frail out here on the streets. His face pockmarked and pale, his mouth attempting a smile but contorted in dismay. Julian tastes metal and the circle closes in. Davis stands at attention unmoving, and before thought has time to contradict, Julian salutes. Sweat trickles down Julian's neck as a flood of memories and sensations cascade through his body; the strength of those days, the strength of purpose and the pressure of life and death; the paradox of saving lives and killing and how he wanted it to be over then and how anymore he wishes it had never ended, aches for some way to return, spinning in that watery place, consumed with importance and meaning.

So we both made it out alive. So what? The following days and months were just that, the ones that followed, just days, just months. Trying to hurry them along.

For what he never knew, just hurry and rush standing still.

Julian squats down under the eve against the wall, Davis joins him, neither men speak. There is nothing to say and the flow of unbidden memories is too potent; memories of a time and place where the bonds of friendship were all that held them together and often all that kept them alive; memories of a place that tore them apart and then sent them home in pieces. Some of the pieces had been left in the jungle, others lost upon reentry. There is nothing to hold on to, nothing holding it together. The mind, the body want to fly out in all directions, that's the most frightening thing of all but the men hold on, they know how to hold on and wait it out. Julian pulls out a tobacco pouch from his jacket, rolls a cigarette draws in deeply and watches the smoke curl up and vanish. "Wait it out, wait it out," he whispers, offering the smoke to Davis. Shifting time and timelessness grip the men to an ever increasing degree as memories vivid and alarming wash over them, deafening in the brightness of explosions and turning into physical impacts, into pressure within and without.

"How'd you find me here?" Julian finally asks. "Maybe Illyria, even that's unlikely but you tracked me all the way into my alley. My alley. Spooky."

Davis shifts. Looking down at the wet asphalt, at his wet shoes. His pants are rain splattered and the jacket he wears is wet from shoulder to waist. He is out of place on the streets and doubly out of place in the alley and he feels it.

"It wasn't easy, I'm getting better at it though. Looked up Gutierrez and Franklin from our company already so it's getting easier. My uncle is a private investigator so he gave me tips."

"Tips, hmm. Alley, how'd your uncle figure to find someone in an alley."

"Just say it took a while. But that's not important. I wanted to see you again. Check up on our company. Actually I have a half brother who lives in Illyria so I thought maybe it's fate or destiny, too much of a coincidence anyway. Sorry to find you here like this."

"Fuck 'like this.' It is what it is. I served my country. I'm just not ready to step onto the treadmill just yet, maybe ever. Fuck the treadmill."

"Yeah, just saying, this sucks, Julian. Don't get too used to it."

Julian's silence is all the answer Davis needs to know he's stepped over a line.

Davis doesn't hear Julian stand, he only sees movement as Julian walks off toward 4th Avenue.

"Wait up. I didn't mean anything by that."

"Fuck 'that,' it's cold here, I need to move around."

"My brother lives near here, on Alder, we can hang out, warm up by the fire. You could crash there, at least for tonight."

Julian and Davis step out onto 4th Avenue, into the bright lights. A cluster of students block the way as they reach the

University. Both men stiffen, slow their pace, their heartbeat, monitor the group's movement, monitor the area beyond the corner, recon the area.

"It's the crosshairs I miss, the focus," Julian says as they pass the students. "I even miss the hunger, not the thirst though. Most of the time I swear I still smell the war, brings it all back. Warriors, we were warriors then. What do they know anyway?" Not one of the students notice them as they pass by, to them the two young men in shabby rainsoaked clothes are invisible.

Lily

❖

Therefore if any man be in Christ he is a new creature: old things are passed away; behold all things are become new."   I Corinthians 5:17

Liam stands before the fireplace, dwarfed by the maw of stone and wood and fire. Flames flicker behind him. Backlit by fire as he strides back and forth he is larger than life. He is in his element before the people who believe his every breath is ordained by God. This land is his kingdom, these people his flock; his sheep, his lambs.

He looks out at the faces staring back at him. The young faces of his flock, young men and women, mostly in our teens. He nods and lingers, looking at those who sit near him at the front. And then to us at the far wall, near the windows.

Liam nods to a man and woman sitting off to the side waiting for his cue. The woman plays a guitar, strums chords to an old gospel song, then they begin a harmony and we join in singing softly, eyes half closed in trancelike ecstasy. Singing, knowing ours is the kingdom of God. Knowing we are the chosen ones. When the singing stops Liam holds the silence with his eyes.

"To look back," he whispers, "means to return to the old I Am. Christ talks about putting new wine into old wineskins . . . what happens?" He whispers into the silence. "The wine bursts the old wineskins and then there is neither wine nor wineskin. Both are lost."

Liam wipes his face with a white handkerchief. He moves away from the fireplace toward the large windows facing the barns, the pasture and the woods, looks out into the pitch black darkness of night.

"Somewhere out there are our brothers, Marty and Sawyer. I don't know their reasons but they walked away from the Lord today. Walked off in full view of the brethren waiting to get started on a long hard work day. Sawyer in his strength, Marty in his youth. An innocent, a babe in Christ, following a man not the Holy Spirit.

Liam's anger is unleashed, full and threatening, like a parent's rejection. His forgiveness, if it comes, is like grace flooding a torn and broken heart. But waiting for his forgiveness is torture and gnawing. Again he scans the faces before him in the silence, allows the rebuke to settle in. It is scriptural to reject the backsliders in our midst. Insubordination is too great a threat to the unity of the group. Not that which comes from without but that which comes from within.

"Like the early church in the Book of Acts we choose to live our lives in communion with God's Holy Spirit. Amen?"

"Amen."

Liam points to Paul and two other brothers, calls them to the front, asks if there are any who need healing. Beside me, Mary lifts her head from the cap she is crocheting, tentatively stands and walks to the front. Mary is kind, everything about her is an expression of kindness, her soft and easy smile her generosity, her self sacrifice. Like a pixie she moves among the brethren helping wherever she can and comforting those who are struggling. She confesses she's been under condemnation, unable to trust the Lord's forgiveness and asks for strength and healing.

The men make a circle around her, lay hands on her shoulders, her head. Liam closes his eyes prays in tongues then in English, asks for spiritual healing, for forgiveness, for renewed trust in the forgiveness of God. The tension of going up in front of the brethren, of asking for prayer brings on a coughing spell. The spasm lasts minutes and while Mary coughs the men simply stand in prayer making no attempt to assist. I go to the kitchen for a glass of water for Mary. Soon the coughing subsides and Mary returns to her place beside me on the bench.

"How embarrassing." Mary looks down at her hands, a small spray of blood stains them. She quickly rubs them on her skirt looking sideways at me in case I saw. I catch her eye, hold it. "Don't tell," Mary whispers.

"What?"

"I don't want to be sent away. I can't go home, I'll lose my salvation there. I know it, I will, I can't hold on without being here. She picks up the cap, almost completed, begins to pull out the stitches, rewind the yarn back onto the ball, carefully, silently.

Mary

❖

In the stillness after the Bible study thoughts flow in and take shape beside the crochet hook, the black, red, yellow and white yarn I reclaimed from a sweater. Yarn for a hat for my father. Colors form pictures and feelings, colors of feelings. Black holds everything in check like a barrier or even bumpers a way of bounding like the Holy Spirit. A blackness that also comforts. Womblike darkness - protective. Red is strong vital, the passion and compassion of Christ. Yellow softens the other colors in a kind of confusion but at the same time somehow holds potential. White blinds, it is too bright for the eye to see and shifts to black darkness as soon as it appears. There is a fickleness with white, shifty ungrounded and too quick. I like red the best I am at home there.

   A clap of sound and shockwaves pass through, reverberate through my body. A piece of wood slipped from Bernie's arms and I am returned from my reverie. Everyone is gone but Bernie. I should get up and go but instead I watch. Bernie moves like a ghost, hardly visible, but always working, keeping the fire just right, gathering, hauling, chopping; cleaning out the ashes, mountains of ashes, tending, tending. He bows slightly in apology and goes back to work.

The fire atop glowing coals is small now and intimate. The Lord whispers, *wash Bernie's feet*, a clear voice in my heart. *See my servant, wash his feet.* My heart sinks, fear rushes up. A fear of foolishness of putting myself forward, of looking the fool. Return to the safety of blackness, the protection of the womb, solitude, safety. No, no, no no. *This is my faithful servant. Wash his feet.* I close my eyes, no, no, no. But I must.

I am only going to the kitchen for a bowl of warm, soapy water. I am not washing his feet. I am bringing a washcloth and towel to the fire. I am bringing oil to the fire. I am not washing his feet.

Bernie looks surprised when I tell him the Lord wants me to wash his feet. Humbled he sits on one of the chairs nearest the fire and removes his shoes and socks. Broken shoes, mudstaineds socks. I kneel before him take his foot in my hand, wash gently, warm soapy water gently easing the dirt from toes and soles, easing the long day from tired feet. Physical cleansing, spiritual honoring. I dry his foot, rub oil from the kitchen, start on the other foot. Afterwards we pray, me still kneeling on the wood floor, Bernie still in his chair. Closing my eyes I speak to the Lord my commitment to him, my gratefulness that I have been called as his servant, my gratitude for Bernie's sacrifice. A hand on my shoulder and I look up. Bernie's hands are in his lap. The Lord has honored me with his touch.

Sawyer

❖

It takes a careful hand and a sharp knife to really open her up. Marty's job is to hold her hind legs apart, back to the ground, stomach up and centered. With my knife between two fingers and my palm away from her belly, careful not to nick anything inside, a long slit down the abdomen opens the belly and the intestines fall out steaming and reeking. I plunge my bare hands in deep, up to the elbows, carefully pull out the long purple and white tubes of the intestines then dig for the lungs, the heart. Covered in blood.

Memories flood in, memories of childhood, good days with my father, my brothers, the backwoods, the hunt for our sustenance. Can't help it, smiling, laughing, talking non stop. The Lord brought me here for just this one thing, providing for the people. He knew it all along. Then easy, easy and she opens up to me. And now her on her side I reach into her body with both hands deeper and deeper until I can cut away her diaphragm and then her windpipe. While Marty holds her ribs open I tug and cut from her throat downward bringing everything out, little by little, cutting organs away from ribs. I do the one side then we flip her and do the other. Back and forth like a dance, my arms submerged in her body, submerged in blood, my face pressed up against her open wound, reaching farther and farther in until I'm able to completely separate her organs and her intestines from the walls of the ribcage. Then the liver comes out, dense, blood saturated. Now's the moment of reverence, the silent moment of gratitude that this elk gave her life for us. That the Lord brought her to us.

I slice off a thin strip for Marty, holding it out for him to take, myself holding the dripping lobe to my mouth. "This is the hunter's reward, the strength, the spirit resides in the liver - eat." I bury my face in the bloody slab, come away chewing, dripping blood. Marty's face is white. "Marty, Marty my little virgin eat. You'll like it, it'll make a man out of you, trust me. The first bite is sweet. It's always sweet then it changes because time changes everything but the first bite is always sweet."

I miss the carnage of the hunt. Truth is, I miss the carnage of war. This way of Christianity bypasses war and mostly hunting but I carry it inside me and I miss it. We say turn the other cheek but that's why Liam has it over on us. He's the last one to turn a cheek but no one notices that. He's held to a different standard or rather he's not held to any standard. Looking at him it's not possible to actually see him - see who he is, what he is. War is like that. After the man becomes a soldier, he becomes a war machine. We see what we're told to see, what we're allowed to see, vision changes, the man changes. The man becomes who he was intended to be, made whole by the force of war, without the confusion of the details of life - the confusion of woman who wants us to become something civilized, domesticated, the machine of peace. Maybe I just miss that too much, the war machine. If Liam told us to go to battle maybe then I'd respect him more. It's like we're waiting for the sign to do it but we don't know what 'it' is. How many months did we study Revelations? The last days are here, it's close to being over and done, we already know that, just like in war, it's always close to being done; death is a heartbeat away that's what makes it singular but here we're not allowed to bludgeon, plunder or rape. The opposite, we're celibate, we're polite, we forgive or say we do. I feel like blowing someone's brains out. God, I feel good.

"Tastes sweet," Marty says.

"That's right, you got it."

And the Old Testament, one big justification for war once they crossed into the Promised Land. What could be more promising than justified mass slaughter? First thing. First thing after they cross over, what do they do? *And they utterly destroyed all that was in the city, both man and woman, young and old, and ox, and sheep, and ass, with the edge of the sword.* Joshua 6:21

Ha! But we always gloss over that. Now we say it's about sin and forgiveness. Endless forgiveness but back then they're out there slaughtering everything that moves.

"You have a knife back in your tent?" Marty looks up from his strip of liver. Shakes his head. "You need to carry one, now you're initiated into the hunt. Part of your equipment, part of your world. Knife'll make you know who you are, change who you are, even if you never get a chance to use it. Just havin' it on your hip makes the difference. Take me for example, I always carry mine and if I hadn't we'd a been out here without a weapon. No weapon, no hunt."

"The sword of the Lord." Marty says. "I carry my Bible like that. Feels like completion when I'm out on the street sharing the Lord. Hunting. Ha, never thought of it like that but it's like hunting. The world may be lost and the people lost but getting out there and evangelizing brings it back to me of why I'm here. The taste of bringing someone to the Lord - sweet. Feeling that love and completion, that resting place of joining the ministry, or rather of coming to the Lord. And now it's learning to be a vessel, it's my body that's the enemy. It's the enemy most times. We talk about Satan but it's here inside me that the real battle happens. The sword of the Lord and Jesus. Purity and clarity. Everything else has to go by the wayside. Praise the Lord."

"Praise the Lord."

I like Marty, he's full of the Spirit still.

"Reminds me of when I was baptized in the Holy Spirit," Marty says. "That total immersion in the Spirit, that moment when it all flooded over me, when tongues was the only way I could even express the beauty of it. I wanted to howl like a wolf but held back. Can you imagine that? If I'd howled? Ha, what a trip but that was in my throat just then. I was in the basement at the 10th Street house in town, in Illyria, and the brothers and sisters who were there all came down and put their hands on me. Completely covered me in their prayers, surrounded me like a cloud praying and talking in tongues. I'd never felt anything like it before. What was it like for you when you got baptized in the Holy Spirit?"

"Not like that, ha! I was baptized when I was a kid. It was all part of the whole family thing so I didn't actually know what it was but I went along with it because my brothers were doing it. Back home we - not just my family but everyone I knew - were into the church. Pentecostals, the whole valley was Pentecostals. It was good, the singing and the praying. Mostly as a kid I liked the shouting. We got to shout a lot. Hallelujah! Fun stuff. Then we'd go hunting. That was the real religion . . . Then Nam. That was hunting and being hunted. Both. At the same time. Being on edge day an' night for months, there's no end jus' the sunrise and sunset, the smell of the men: War changes you, thinking about your buddies beside you in a different way. And the smell of your gun. Metal, oil, taking it apart, cleaning, assembling. You're different, not so much thinking about what's going on around you or what's next but sensing, reacting like a machine. I became an extension of my gun, not the other way around like you'd think. A machine, like the gun I carried then."

"You drafted?"

"No, enlisted. Wanted to move on, time to get out of our valley and do something else. Plus I wanted war. Wanted the real hunt. Now we're taught to turn the other cheek and war seems like the opposite of that but it ain't. I ain't going' to justify how I went to war on purpose. I needed to and that's enough.

"Yeah, we're soldiers of the Lord just without the weapons."

"If you say so."

"I got a deferment. Ate a bunch of Twinkies before my physical and they thought I was diabetic. Didn't do it on purpose but that's how it turned out. I was glad. Actually I was planning to go to Canada but turned out I didn't have to."

"You wouldn't have lasted out there, trust me."

Julian

❖

The light shifts as the moon appears from behind the clouds. The small University neighborhoods are lit by yellow street lamps most of which are out or alternately off and on and most of which give off little light even when lit. The University huddles inward, surrounded by a ring of small houses, a graveyard, downtown, and the river sliding westward on the north side. On the eastern edge a freeway cuts a great gash into the ring and opens up to Springer and the stinking exhaust billowing out of lumber mills.

Watching Davis from behind, the back, the narrow shoulders, the uneven posture, my eyes again see what they saw in Nam, those same shoulders between myself and that floating grenade. Couldn't take my eyes off that grenade then. I watched it drift on the wind like a bird poised to strike a fish just beneath the surface of the waters. Saw this back, these shoulders turn and then it was Davis threw himself at me that last possible moment.

The house is near the University, an old bungalow from the 1940's. Old maples line the sidewalks and overhang the streets, lavender bushes and juniper nestle beside the porch. Dim light from within and smoke rising up out of the fireplace promise warmth. In the front room a few musical instruments are carefully placed in a corner. A stained, worn couch is on the far wall and a couple old chairs face the fire.

Standing before the fire, we watch the flames rise and dance. Davis talks about his new life. Some words about God penetrate then fade out again. Hearing is tricky now and words can't always be trusted. Something about Jesus but then that could have been an expletive.

A young man comes out of the back room.

"My brother," Davis says, nodding toward the newcomer.

Lee takes the long way around the chairs, careful to not step between myself and the fire, reaches out to shake hands.

"I'm Lee," he says respectfully. "Don't mind my brother, he never learned his manners."

Lee's dark skin against Davis' pale whiteness, Lee's jet black hair long against Davis' blond military cut.

"I'm Julian. Ahó." The word comes out instinctively and once said I look into Lee's eyes for recognition. Lee nods then and the recognition is acknowledged, wordless recognition of family and tribe, n'dn way. Then Davis stumbles back into view and abruptly opens his mouth sputtering something that I can't understand and don't want to hear. The word sounds mangle in this man's throat the way I feel mangled in this man's presence. But why? We lived and breathed that time, that air together. Watched soldiers die, and killed like all warriors must. Davis couldn't help that he was white, a man with the baggage of conqueror, history maker, Savior. Because Davis saved my life? And we were ever after connected, savior and saved? My life a mirror of all the hated false history the conquerers had written? But in Davis' presence all sense of self blurs. Who I am, who my relatives are, were, my culture, all blurred.

Nightly in the alley I reconstructed myself, building that sense of home and tribe from within, an internal place that I hoped would carry me. But it was a fragile business and easily undone. I stayed away from the rez, told myself I was taking a break. But

I knew without knowing I couldn't take the chance of finding out that the last thread linking me to my people was broken. So I hung on in the unlikely place of Illyria, white college town, emerald empire, rainforest.

Watching Lee, Lee and Davis catching up, a long lost childhood remembered. Suburbs in the 1950s in Southern California. A time of sheltered freedom, of safe and free afternoons on manicured lawns and idyllic games in the evenings until the street lights came on, of neighborhood barbecues and long carefree summers.

Like shadows seen from the outside of a teepee cast by the little fire in the center, memories come into view, unbidden reminders of what seems lost; simple days with cousins running barefoot and free, laughing into the night, sitting beside campfires out near the river alone or with Grandma. Remembering the language of fires and the way of the spirit nation called fire. Companions everywhere - the fire nation, the stone nation, the green and growing, the creepy crawlies, the wingeds, the four leggeds.

Summers were long and carried their own kind of freedom. A freedom born of benign neglect, I always said. The reservation houses were built in tidy even rows based on the suburb model but the neglect there was deliberate and angry. And instead of evening barbecues, parents gathered inside, in rooms empty of furniture save an old couch taken from a dumpster too many winters ago and refrigerators empty of food but for the small tub of lard on the top shelf. Government checks came regularly and then there was celebration and celebration meant beer or maybe something harder. The initial festivity always turned bad and hateful and violent. I stayed away on those days.

Those days the cousins would join Grandma at the river and stay there for as many days as it took to spend the government's money. Grandma refused to speak the white man's language and she refused to move into the white man's house. On nights when she wasn't dragged back to the house to sleep on the bed they said was hers she stayed in a small teepee by the river. The cousins gathered around her fire and we all listened to stories of the old days in the old language. Stories of the Buffalo nation and the hunts that lasted for many days and sometimes weeks. Stories of travel when winter was approaching and the whole camp would pick up and leave nothing behind to show they had ever been there. We learned our native tongue from Grandma and swore to each other on oath that we would keep the stories and the old ways and never drink and never take the government's money.

Lee disappears, returns with a joint and offers it to Davis, offers it to me. Davis waves it off, mumbling something about sobriety. And again the word Jesus.

Lee laughs, "you still claiming you're straight?"

"More for us then," I say. "You mind?" I ask, nodding in the direction of the drums.

"No, Let's do this, but first this," he smiles passing the joint to me.

From my seat behind the drum I can see the fire. Tentative at first, mechanical and distant with too much effort to chase something, to hold or capture something but then gradually, softening the effort, loosening my focus, my control, a rhythm emerges. Moments stretch into minutes and this dance, this relationship, this kinship to the fire and the drum returns.

Lee moves behind an old cello and begins to pull notes deep and resonant that blend with the drum in ways I did not think possible. Together we play to the rhythm of the flame, music that feels ancient, coming from the sacred the way the songs have always come to our people. Catching the rhythms with deep tones and rhythmic pauses Lee looks to the flame, softens his focus, connects to the drum, connects to the fire. Then closing his eyes he follows the drum, now the sound of a heartbeat coming from deep within the earth.

In my hearing then in my voice a song comes, an old song, a song come up from dreamtime and remembered, passed down through the generations. Vocables, the sound of water, pure and cleansing replace the images of war with the sound of water burbling over stones.

Mni Wakan Olowan, Sacred Water song, held inside this

song, safely held as I open throat to voice, to vocables in the ancient tongue. Four directions song, bringing in the spirits song, the fire now a sheet of dancing color. I haven't heard these songs since before army days. Tears falling. This music, this fire, these tears are all, all I am right here, right now.

Davis at the couch, listens from the outside. He has always listened from the outside. Lee now singing like a war chief, indecipherable words rising in his throat from someplace Davis has never heard, never accessed. Davis, eyes wide, fearstates swallowing him, listens to the drum and the cello and our voices calling to the spirits. Familiar, n'dn way, but unfamiliar to Davis and he reacts to these songs the way I react to discordant, arhythmic jazz.

"Why must there always be breakdown? Why not just a crack?" He whispers. "Famous last words. 'There's a crack in everything - that's how the light gets in.' Ha Leonard, easy for you to say, the whole of them dying, sinking deeper and deeper into the black earth, seeds seeking the depths wanting to sprout. Easy for you to say. What if there is no sprouting, only decay? Well, well, that's a fine mess you've gotten us into, isn't it Ollie? But the beat goes on. Why does the beat go on? Fuck the beat, fuck it, fuck it. Fuck it, fuck it, fuck it."

Suddenly Davis is calling out what, moments before, was only a whisper. Lee watches his brother swing his arms in defiance against an unseen foe.

"Yeah, fuck it," I call out, adding my voice to Davis', calling out louder, more ferocious, more threatening. "Fuck. It."

His eyes say I am a stranger to him, no longer his fellow in the field. A warrior from some ancient, far off time who doesn't belong here. But Davis' dreamstate shatters in the sudden silence and in an instant, Davis' eyes soften. Again he sees something solid, a buddy pushing against an unseen, a common, foe. Standing with him against whatever comes.

"We got this. You got this. I think we need more wood for the fire. Lee you think we need more wood?"

"Yeah, it's out on the side of the house. I'll get it."

Davis watches out of the corner of his eye. The fragile trust already gone, a cold shivering in his extremities thrusts him back into a fearstate, one he can't pull out of.

"Watch the fire," I say, carefully placing four small branches on top of the coals. A gentle fire licks up from the wood and warms and lights the room again. I lean in close, stretch my hands to the warmth.

"Come with me back to the fire. It's a good fire, see? Nothing going on here."

The room shimmers then settles to just the fire. Lee returns with more wood and then steps up behind the cello. Davis moves closer to the fire, pushes the burning wood to the side with sticks, shapes the coals in ever changing patterns, working the coals artfully, arranging them first into a circle with rays, then a crescent, then an eagle.

"Where'd you learn that?" I ask.

"Navajo Nation, Lee's people."

"See and all this time I thought you was Wasichu."

"Ha, yeah well, maybe I am."

"You never said nothing. All that time, working the lines and all. Defending each other with our lives. Knowing you had that connection might have made a difference. To me, anyway."

"No reason to bring it up out there, Julian. I, we, were soldiers, that was all. We had to become just that, lose everything else."

"Yeah, you're right about that, lose everything else. Now here we are trying to pick up the pieces. Ship ourselves back in pieces, try to reassemble at the airport. Some task that."

"Reassemble, ha what a joke. More like paste it all together, what didn't get left behind anyway," Davis says.

"But fuck that. Why not get some beer? Either of you have any money?"

Lee steps away from the cello, "I'm for that. Get a case you think? That'll get this night moving. Get something hard to go with it?"

Davis has not spoken up. "You in Davis? You're usually the first one at it."

"I'm trying to clean up."

"You don't sound convinced, man. Come on, let down, celebrate, we got so much to celebrate right? You and me, we made it back and now here we are on solid ground. Hey, and no one's even shooting at us. That's enough reason to celebrate. Remember that time on LSD? The land shimmered and the enemy came at us looking like elves, Santa's elves. What a shit storm and we lived. Come on, man just this once. Go straight tomorrow."

Lily

❖

The sisters sleep in a huge army tent a short trail away from the dining hall. It smells of wood smoke and kerosene. Black flowers of mold grow up along the sides of the canvas. Twenty bunks, some flat against the walls, some pointing in toward the wood stove create little alleys, the illusion of a small town. Thirty-four sisters in one tent, the bodies alone should warm it some but they only add to the moisture.

It is a dense chill, a dense, moist chill that finds its way past clothing, skin and muscle and touches bone. Teeth grind, muscles cramp and this is only November. Women move quickly, quickly change into long-johns and thick socks, knit caps, neck wraps; quickly dry brush teeth, quickly slide into thin damp sleeping bags that have seen too many winters to keep anyone warm even in summer, stuff sweaters and socks and scratchy dirt crusted jeans in sleeping bags for warmth.

I stoke the fire gridlike to the top with space for air. The wood stove and pipe turn red. Sliding my feet down to the bottom of the sleeping bag I find the sweater I keep there for extra warmth, wrap it around my feet, my toes, focus on the red stove.

Mary in the bunk above me coughs. Long deep in the chest coughing until someone brings her water.

"Do you need anything?" I ask.

"No," she whispers. "The Lord will heal me. Just . . . don't say anything."

"About what"

"This cough, I don't want to be sent back home."

"Why do you say that? No one would send you home for being sick."

"It's just that . . . I can't go home, I'll lose my salvation at home. I know it, I will, I can't hold on without being here. And I want to be strong for the Lord. And a witness too. What does it say about my faith if I can't get over this sickness? How can I be an example of God's miracle if I can't get over this?

"I heard Sawyer and Marty were hunting deer this morning, looking to bring us meat. Like mana, the Lord will provide. Tomorrow we might have meat, that would help us all. Like the Lord Himself put it on our plates. Like mana or the quail only bigger. Fish and loaves from Jesus Himself. I was praying for meat last week, thinking it might not be right, thinking it's selfish to pray for meat, maybe even a sin but now, the Lord gave me a sign, now the Lord will provide and answer my prayer, Praise the Lord."

"Amen, praise the Lord," I say.

A sister leans down from the next bunk over, looks, down at me. "I heard they had bags packed up beforehand and were planning how to run off for the past week. But I don't believe it," she says. "I believe the Lord answered our prayers."

Conversations rise and fall in the dim glow of the lanterns, then darkness and the smell of kerosene as lanterns are blown out. Then silence, then temptation. At this liminal moment temptation comes. Time is our own, thoughts are our own, our bodies let down, disciplined thoughts let go. Dreamstates take over even before the the smell of kerosene fades. The day starts early when we will hold our tongues, hold our thoughts to the perfection of the saints but this in-between time stretches out long, and the breath of temptation is felt. We call it sin. The sin of doubt, the sin of sadness, the sin of complaint, the sweetness of a memory drifting in, all part of our sinful nature.

The dark of night frees and threatens. Some cover their heads, their ears, cover their mouths, wait to fully enter the deep, refusing the possibility of the lingering in-between, allowing only sleep. Others hold out for the few moments given to us when responsibility can be laid at the foot of dreamstates; they savor the safety of the tent and red glowing heat pipe, sleeping bags, and each other. Eventually sleep overtakes but for a fleeting moment, just before darkness falls, all live in a space of unfettered honesty, too tired to fight it, too tired to take on the condemnation born of the day.

Condemnation. 'I am under condemnation' is what we say when faith fails, when hope is gone and all that's left is fatigue and tedium and restlessness; under condemnation because we can't bear the weight of our own nature. Then childmade by words meant to shame into compliance. The promise of God is Salvation, the promise of God is Hell. Which? Both. Easier at first when a bright and glorious sheen surrounded everything and everyone. The brightness of salvation a pure undiminished light more pure than virgin snow, a light so bright eyes could be blinded by it and so the need for an intercessor, and now the visions of Hell stark in my mind. The threat that I had been guided by the hands of the Devil all my years, that my wisdom, my experience was all a cruel trick of twisted evil made palatable by a fallen angel, once the companion of the God and now bent on moving me closer and closer to death, the final victory. So well I knew his voice, that sweet inner voice so clear so understandable. Now I struggle to learn the language of this other, the one we call Lord. The face of Jesus vaguely familiar, a friend I had once known, had written poetry with, a soul mate conjured, one who knew me better than I knew myself. So sweet, so very sweet but this other, this Lord God of All, requires learning and a teaching by one who has interpreted it and knows what the Book really means and until then, until the time I know the teachings and can walk upright and with a pure heart, I look to Liam.

Tony waiting, nods and I mount. No bridle, no saddle, his ears aflame we gallop toward the woods, past Liam's trailer. They can't see me but I can see them. Brothers out working. Hardly see who's who for the shadows everywhere. In the forest the shadows turn into faces. Faces everywhere watching and staring. Then in an instant they're gone and in their place the trees rise up and sing. Foreign voices tree voices, sometimes the sound of a heart beat. Sometimes a single note. Then sweet sounds - way ya, hey ya - soothing voices a harmony coming from the trees in their language, their tongues. Speaking in tongues the woods filled with the Holy Spirit. Way ya, hey ya.

Deep in the forest a pitchy darkness covers like a shroud, inky sticky darkness so black it shines white. Tony's ears aflame, delicate yellow, orange and white flickers. Branches haphazard grab with brash fingers, tear at our eyes, Tony's and mine. The deadwood forest crumbles beneath Tony's hooves, the sky above, a broken gash, a scar between the slanting firs. We follow the lost river to the south, its burbling soothing song gently guiding us forward. We leave the river for higher ground, the forested hillside, then back down into gaping canyons then back up onto the scaly mountain top - the grey granite cliffs overlooking the valley and suddenly we are free. Down below the river glitters, a silver thread in the bright darkness.

Tony stops, this is his place, his tree, his grass. He snorts long and forceful, lowers his head to graze. I slide off, step out onto the ledge, a granite rock cliff that juts out over a great crevasse of open space.

Down below the lost river babbles, Ululu, Ululu. Upward and on all sides a great virgin forest rises, thousands upon thousands of fir trees, lush, green, verdant; upturned spikes, rising straight, sharp and immovable. I step onto the ledge, look out over the vast carpet of green, breathe in, filling lungs filling lungs, resist the urge to leap, the almost irresistible urge. Squat on my haunches. Down, down resting my hands on the rough, cool stone, lean out, lean out. My free will, the temptation of Christ, the temptation of the devil. Scraping hands in solidarity with palms, broken pierced palms. Solidarity. Blood flows red from the rocks, seeps down, finds the river below. Now red, it sings, Ululu, Ululu. 'Free fall, flow river flow On and on it goes Breathe underwater 'till the end.'

Someone, a man, my savior? clings to a tree down below and stretches his hand out to meet mine, inviting the end? "This is the End," he croons, then laughs at me, pointing and accusing that I've left my soul behind. A swarm of crows circle overhead, spiral down the river valley echo back to the waters Ululu, Ululu. Goodbye friend I call out as he joins the crows.

Deep labored breathing and the odor of mansweat from behind. I turn. Karl, one of the brothers, steps out from behind the trees, he stands beside Tony strokes his neck. Tony moves away, pins his ears back. The man lowers his hood and speaks. "They won't like finding you out here. Finding out you're up here all alone," he says. "You know we don't do that. Two by two, that's how we do. It. You know that. Shouldn't be here like this and that in the dark of night. Might as well come back down, save yourself the crucible of explaining."

Norse code, he speaks in rhymes. Tells stories from behind curly blond beard long blond to this chest, hair of spun gold. But I, singing, explain that here on this mountain we can find the very edge of salvation, see the hand of God and return blissfully alive to tell the tale. Sweetness and light surround the land below illumined by a moon that shafts down in lightspears through the silver clouds.

"Look there," I whisper. "That man is gaining on the crows and will lead them the next time around. You'll see. There's more to salvation than obedience.

There's beauty and wonder. Kindness."

"Woman," he booms out through a silver megaphone. "Hold your tongue. 'I suffer not a woman to speak or to usurp authority over a man.' Do you deign to teach me. A Man. You, a woman, teach? That will not be. That can not be."

The man swoops past, laughing. The crows follow. A murder of crows. I duck down. The brother, cursing, reaches up and tries to capture one by the leg and misses, almost losing his footing at the brink. He calls out something but I can't understand the words.

"You," he hisses, pointing at my chest, looking at my breasts, "are in sin and in danger of damnation."

Taking my hand he leads us away from the brink, gently he lays his jacket on the ground, a gentlemanly gesture, then softly speaking gently soothing singsong speaks, "remember your ancestor, Eve, she went out alone in the beauty of the garden, wanting only to find the sweetness of the morning dew on her labors as she walked in Paradise. She took leave of Adam, insisting she would appreciate him even more after absence. And Adam, not wanting her to go objected but she prevailed and finally he agreed. That was the first time woman found her voice, her own authority and we know how that ended. So he partook and they both fell but hers was the greater weakness because even before she ate of the forbidden fruit she had already pulled away that she might stand on her own."

Marty

❖

Clothes wet, soaked through with blood and rain. The fire is going, the coals burn red and pulsate but it's too hot to get up close and too cold not to. Steam rises from our clothes like clouds. The sky clears and the temperature plummets. Open to galaxies of stars above, twinkling in the freezing air, panic closes in.

"It's about to get cold," I say. Sawyer's cock-sure attitude is no match for a deep freeze. "Once the cloud cover goes there's nothing to keep the warm air in - and the clouds just disappeared."

Sawyer looks up, sees the stars, the milky way. "I've been so focused on the fire I had no idea."

"I've been in night freezes after the rains before," I say. "Everything ices. It's colder even than when it snows. You know the hunt but I know our weather and this is about to get serious."

"There's a way of making fires in a ring, smaller ones than this. And then you stay inside the circle. That's one way to keep warm."

"It's one way to stay alive you mean."

"You think it's gonna get dangerous cold tonight, there's a second option." Sawyer looks over at the elk. Its large open cavity a sheltering cave.

"That's the other option," he says. "But if we're even gonna consider it we have to clear this area of the entrails. Out here it's asking for scavengers to just leave it sit. Even if we don't get up inside, even if we try to wait it out by the fire, we need to move this stuff away. The blood smell's gonna attract all kinds of predators."

"We got coyotes here. Cinnamon bears. Wolves are just starting to come back after being decimated by ranchers, I'm glad of that, but not so glad tonight. Coyotes are crafty. They already know we're here. Maybe if we give 'em the guts and some organ meat they'll be satisfied. Last thing I want is to tangle with a pack of coyotes or worse a pack of wolves. I'm glad now we didn't skin her. Makes it harder for them if they do come around."

"We'll have to spook 'em off if, or rather when, they come," Sawyer says. "Tonight's gonna be a long one. We gotta dry these clothes out better too. Things we do for the brethren, eh Marty?"

The forest is dark even with the bit of moonlight. At first I hold a lit branch so Sawyer can see to drag the long stringy guts away from our camp. But it takes both of us to carry it distant enough without breaking or puncturing the delicate tissue surrounding, so we end up dragging in the dark.

Something's gathering in the distance, watching us work. We can't see them in the dark but occasionally one of them stares just right at the fire and the eyes flash. They're pretty quiet but there's this low growl coming from the forest. Eerie low growl. Sawyer slows his pace. "Focus," he says. "Likely they won't attack us. Just nip at the guts."

But one does. A wolf pup jumps at Sawyer who is in front and quick as a flash Sawyer drops the guts, swings his knife and stabs it even as it lunges toward his shoulder. "Sorry brother," he says to the young wolf.

The rest of the pack scatter then and Sawyer just continues as though nothing happened.

"You okay?" I ask.

"He just grazed my jacket. Hoped I wouldn't have to do that. Definitely we'll need to take them some organ meat. This shit is not tasty no matter how hungry they are. We can scatter this one around too. That'll spook 'em from coming closer. Maybe. It's something my dad used to say, might not be true though. Sometimes when he was drunk he'd say things. Anyway we'll scatter him just in case.

Julian

❖

Julian wakes at first light. He places a few sticks in the fireplace and blows on the coals until a small flame ignites. Outside the sun crests the horizon and its rays spread over the neighborhood bright and clear. It has been a long gloomy stretch of colorless grey and Julian is full of wonder at the sapphire blue overhead and the shadows dark and clearedged. Without thinking he is out the door and walking, icy broken shards crunch underfoot. His first breath, a deep breath that wants to fill the lungs with clear pure air catches, burns.

Huddled against the cold he travels the back alleys and the neighborhoods to the hill above the University, the cemetery above the University. The dead whisper to him in their own various voices and he whispers back. So much easier here among the dead. His Mother came to him in a vision once. She in her death mask spoke clearly, said, "Come to a party, it's okay they're all dead so you don't have to worry about all that other stuff."

From within the canopy of a weeping willow a man emerges,

broken down with age and neglect, swinging a long knife, side to side at some unseen adversary, a hunting knife at least six inches long. He spots Julian, squints, hunches down and lunges, grateful for a flesh and blood target.

"Damn Indian. Get out of my town. You don't belong here. Get out of here. You hear me? I'll tear your heart out and feed it to the pigeons if you stay."

More men emerge from beneath the willows like rats scampering in the night, seeking what crumbs might appear. Then seizing upon Julian as a perfect target for their twisted hunger they move toward him, close in on him. "No, don't go," one of the men croons. "Stay a while, it's okay he was only kidding. Put the knife down Hank, you hear me?"

Fearsmells from the men accost his senses, the ancient stench of fear dismembering his hold on what is. *Hold hard, do not back down*, a disembodied voice speaks.

Clarity and stillness.

Julian runs at the man with the knife, cuffs him on the side of the head, counting coup, runs to the nearest of the other men and does the same. He glares at the others, takes a step toward them, cries out a war whoop and they scatter.

In the solitude of the graveyard, the ghosts sigh and breathe again. Julian takes an old bunch of dried red and white carnations and a broken flag from the grave of Lydia Whitehorse and smoothes the dirt mound near her headstone, resets the flowers, the flag. Leaning against her headstone he recites by memory "A child and daughter, a sister and friend, a wife and mother, a grandmother and a widow. She was loved by many 1879 - 1938."

Julian stirs to the sound of frozen grass crunching under hooves. Or feet. The old man throws the first blow, shattering a branch over Julian's legs. "Stop you in your tracks, you can't walk, Injun Joe." The men laugh as if that was the funniest thing they'd ever heard. Then more blows to his head and back. Then the tall one takes his shoes and beats his soles bloody with a thin branch while the others hold him. Julian struggles to his feet, collapses but once acquainted with his pain, stands again and throws himself at the biggest of the men, the one with his shoes, drags him into the brush, away from Lydia's grave and punches until his fists are bleeding. The other men come up with sticks and pummel Julian from behind.

Soaked, shivering, bloody and shoeless, Julian can't remember where his shoes are or how he lost them, or whose blood this is. There was a house on Alder and a fire and food, warmth and Davis of all people, Davis, but he can't remember where it was or what the house looked like. His knuckles are raw and his feet swollen. He touches his face and can't feel his touch, it's numb and hard and crusted. The empty street stares back at him, morning gulps down his will, the potential of the day gone. With cold stale effort he simply walks.

The neighborhood surrounding the cemetery gives way to the University neighborhood and the foot traffic increases. The shop keepers roll up tin barricades and a big truck stopped in the middle of the street obstructs traffic while a man unloads fresh vegetables and beer. The woman who runs the deli at the corner near campus scowls at him. Students stare and look away quickly, catching themselves at the last possible moment. He can't feel his feet in the frozen morning and his shivering increases uncontrollably. A young woman, a student? stops him, blocking his way. She wears a long skirt and a stocking cap over long blond hair. He thinks she must be a vision. Her smile passes through him like an elixir and he lets out a huge sigh.

"Do you need help?" she asks. The words seem foreign, his hearing is muted and he can't be sure what she said but her face tells him she is not a threat. He lets her guide him into the warmth of a small auxiliary room within the Student Union. Listens as she whispers to a young man who leaves and then quickly returns with shoes, soft warm socks and a washcloth and warm water to cleanse his wounds. She presses a cup of hot coffee into his hands and steps back to observe his brokenness.

Another young man enters to witness the rescue then another young woman. They seem happy to help, happy to find one in need of help. Happy, happy. Julian is too cold to care. Another young man comes with food and more coffee. Just eat and warm up then go. *It's too easy here, soldier. Arm yourself for duty and report to me at o-eight hundred hours.* Yes sir. But he doesn't get up and he doesn't leave and the hackles finally retreat into some unknown corner.

"We live nearby in a house on 10th Street, all of us, and we have 40 acres of land to the east, past Grey Willow. You're welcome at our house if you want." She speaks when the others leave the room, a conspiracy? but then the men return and repeat her offer.

"I'm Julian." Reaching out with his bruised hand he sees it for the first time in the garish brightness of fluorescent bulbs. Sees the blood on his jacket. "Hmm. Can't say I remember all this, he laughs."

"Really, you're welcome at our house. There are extra beds, rooms for the men - we eat good too."

"What's your thing, why are you helping me?" Suspicion clings to him, these white people offering to save him but what he really wants is for the blond to just keep talking.

"We live by the word of God. That's all."

"Nah, thanks for the food and the clothes and all but I'm not religious that way."

"None of us are - that way," she says sitting down beside him. "We just do it. Living like in the early days, we have all things in common and no one needs for anything. We give to anyone in need and feed the hungry. That's all, we just give because the more we give the more comes back to us. We give away our cloak if someone needs it. Or our shoes," she says. "Come to the house and you'll see."

"Can't do that."

"Sure you can." One of the men steps up and holds himself at attention, military attention. His hair too is suspiciously blond and he has the familiar square jaw of a lifer, the piercing stare, the tight, square build.

"Can't do that soldier." Julian repeats.

Lily

❖

The sisters are up early, moving around in semi-darkness. Light from a lantern shows from the far end of the tent. They rush about, dressing in layers, quickly leave the frigid cold of the tent for the warmth of the dining hall. The sky is clear, the trees are covered with hoar frost to the trunks, a winter wonderland without the snow. Everyone moves with a hurried desperation. Something in the bones, a whiplash from some unknown source.

    The dining hall quiet, too quiet. The fireplace stacked high and flames rise to the top of the huge opening but it just breaks the chill in the large room. I pull inside myself, hold to my innermost being, in a survival mode I have not experienced since when I was on the road. It is instinctual, a movement against what? I don't know. Then the flames from the fireplace mingle with the flames from Maggie's ears, the crows, the man above the trees flying and then Karl. The harsh, cold severity of his commands. The rigid icy certainty of his worldview. He wants to marry me but I will never marry him.

The brothers are also up and eating early. Those nearest the fireplace move away so others can take their place and get warm. Like ripples the men change seats without speaking and now that the sisters are joining with their own bowls of oatmeal the brothers move away from the heat of the fire for them. Steam rises from bowls, some eat, others just cradle the bowl in their hands, warming numb fingers, some place their faces over the bowls, breathing in the steam warming someplace deeper. Tears run down my face and awaken me to the fact that I am weeping. Mary comes over and we hug a long time. I have no idea what's going on, what's wrong.

"We were freezing in our sleep," she says. "The temperature plummeted during the night, something like 30 below, and the brothers in the pup tents and us out in the mess tent were slowly freezing."

"How's that possible, I didn't feel cold? I don't know what I felt, just woke up disoriented and . . . hollow. Just that, hollow."

"That's what happens when you're freezing to death, you go numb and then it feels good, like slipping off. Easiest thing in the world to freeze to death."

The mirror image of the frog in the pot of water. Mary rubs her hands together, still trying to rub out the numb. At the table we eat in silence, the food warming us, drink rose hip tea, hot and steaming.

This morning the rising sun flashes broken rays across the pasture, visible from the dining hall, and the grey dawn gives way to clear blue skies. In one movement we all look toward the windows and breathe in the beauty of our land under clear skies. Then Liam steps through the dining hall doors and we all, in one movement turn to watch him line up with the brothers and sisters for breakfast. I've never seen him in the morning, no one has ever seen him eat with us in the morning. The silence in the dining hall thickens as the significance of his presence sinks in. He takes his bowl of oatmeal and cup of tea to a table at the far edge of the hall, away from the heat of the fire, and digs in, eating in silence with the rest of us.

Brothers finished with their breakfast begin to leave and get ready for the workday as usual but Liam stands up and stops them. "Wait, stay inside, I want to talk to you all before we start the day. This isn't an ordinary day and we need to slow down a bit, address what we just went through. Please, sit down," Liam instructs. "Get seconds and there's plenty of rose hip tea that the sisters harvested last summer. Last night was cold and tonight we'll put the sisters in with the married couples, the brothers in the men's dorm. Stay, relax, today we take in what the Lord has given us. Remember the blessings.

"Look around you at what we have accomplished through our faith in the Lord, through his hand upon us and through our obedience to His Word. And you know we sin against the Lord when we fail to see his hand. It's our lack of faith betrays us in moments when we are tested, and tested we were. Not one of us anticipated the drop in temperatures last night, it came upon us unawares by the hand of God and we stand now at the far side of a test. How did we fare? Where are our hearts this morning now that we've actually been through the fire? We come away this morning thankful and glad the Lord has given us the opportunity to feel the test of His hand." Liam looks around the room, unmistakable compassion in his eyes while scanning the faces of each one of us. Judging our faith by the quickness of our 'Amen,' the unhesitant nods of agreement. His benevolent generosity strengthens us as we see again the hand of the Lord all around us.

"He protected us from harm and brought us through this trial of faith because he is a faithful God. And like the Children of Israel walking through the wilderness we have our physical trials. Trials of hunger and lack in so many forms. Today's trial is easy, it's clear, definable, it is objective; it even has roots with the physical tribulations of our brethren who crossed the wilderness for forty years. Though in those days they suffered heat and thirst while we suffer cold. We say we suffered cold for one night and we did. But this morning we praise the Lord because He calls us to sacrifice, He calls us to make our bodies a temple of the Holy Spirit, He calls us to lay down our lives."

A subtle shift moves through the back of the room where

the brothers sit as a group. Where moments before were expressions of confusion and fear now the brothers relax into the holiness of our collective walk with God, the privilege of this moment sinks in as Liam continues to share. Andrew wipes tears from his eyes and bows his head in prayer. These are the holy men who never veer from the path of righteousness and never faint in the face of adversity. Liam nods to the men.

Just after breakfast Liam comes out to the horse barn, says I need to go out on one of the horses, track down those two - Sawyer and Marty - finish the feeding then go. He's still angry but seems more worried this morning.

Maggie is the better horse to use for tracking. She isn't spooky anymore and she's not in foal. Unfortunately she's young and still unreliable. Her time in the woods is limited but for a quarter horse she's solid and better than most three year olds. The first part of the trail is wide, it opens up from the pasture at the near end, then at the far end it crosses into BLM land.

I can easily see the broken earth where the elk were startled. It goes as far as the deer trails that branch off the main trail just below the BLM border. A mess. A churned up, deep and muddy mess. The rains had stopped in the afternoon and now with the freeze the ground seems petrified, impressed with the latest footprints.

Sawyer's and Marty's footprints show up on the edge, like they were following and trying not to get mired down at the same time. Sawyer's a tracker, I'm not but I like the chance to try. The broken branches here are obvious and the churned tracks a child could follow.

Maggie's breath pours like smoke from her nostrils. It fills the air in front of us with little clouds. Her thick winter coat is soft, keeps her warm but my coat is thin and my thin leather riding gloves do nothing to shield me from the cold. Fingers rigid and unbending are not much use for anything other than maintaining a gross kind of contact with the reins. We keep to the icy trail until it thins out and the ground becomes solid and rocky. The ridge is up ahead and that's where some real skill will be needed.

Outside the canopy of the forest the sky opens up, a deep blue sapphire sky. The ridge faces west, looking out over a stretch of forest that goes on to the horizon. Firs like sharp blades to the horizon. Directly below is the reflection of a snaky narrow river, silver in the sun's reflection. Stopping to take it all in, my ears quickly become attuned to the absence of footfalls and jeans rubbing against leather. Silence but for the distant sound of a soft wind moving through the trees and the faint burble of water down below. That is all.

I call out over the ledge into the vastness, "Marty. Sawyer." I listen but there is no response. From here there is no sign of elk or footprints from the brothers. A tree back from the ledge serves as a hitching spot for Maggie and a large flat rock at the edge serves as a bench. Then beside the rock, cigarette butts. Several and fresh.

The trail is invisible from the top, from here it looks to be a sheer descent. On foot I walk the edge; back and forth until I've seen it from all angles. Beyond some large rocks the slightest impression of a trail begins. If I can get Maggie to go that far. She isn't seasoned on the trails. She's hardly seasoned under saddle. The scrape of hooves on granite rock, the image of us slipping, of sliding down, all the way down to the river reverberates in my body. Falling on granite, sliding on granite, I haven't the nerve nor the dexterity to even try. I know they're down there but I can't do it.

Condemnation is a heavy burden. Failure in the sight of God is sin and sin means Hell and I can't find a way out of this. I can't. Men's lives are in jeopardy and I can't do this. Cold sweat runs down my face mixed with tears. The ride back is heavy, weighted. This is a great failure in the sight of God, in the duty to help my brothers. I am in sin.

Julian

❖

I join some others at a table inside the New World coffee house. Schwartz laughs when he sees the torn clothes, bruises, the bits of grass and leaves, the blood.

"I see you've been out sleeping under the stars again. When are you going to learn to sleep indoors? Here, eat the rest of this sandwich. You need it more than I do." Schwartz is a small man, a beady eyed man, fashions himself after a professor. Tweed and blue jeans, a turtleneck, he hands over the crust end of a sandwich.

"This is not so funny. I'm freezing here."

"No, you're feeling sorry for yourself. Time you got your shit together, bro."

"Like you got your shit together? Like Mommy and Daddy paying your rent and tuition while you pretend to go to class? Is that what you mean? Bro?"

"Yeah, well . . . "

"Your dream world doesn't include but a little slice of what is, and that slice is false. A narrow view into a beautiful garden but what you don't see is the broken and destroyed wasteland it took to give you your garden. Fuck you Schwartz and fuck your garden. It isn't my garden and that's okay, I don't want it. I don't want any part of it."

"Hey man, I was just playing with you. Don't walk away."

Outside the cold is harsh and biting, better than sitting with the enemy though. But there are those who know. And also friends who never knew the safety of the scope and the backdrop of chaos but who understand with a look or a nod what's what and 'there it is.' Friends who welcome the long northern night and who are waiting for something, something. But the wait is too long, too white. The asphalt and the concrete stare up from the ground mocking. It is too much, too much and time to leave for True North. South Dakota. The rez. But the snow doesn't melt until May. The relatives would be welcoming but the violence, the drugs and alcohol, the young suicides - what do asphalt and concrete have to say about that? The dirt streets, the muddy rutted streets, the trash and the daily deceptions, the alcoholic mind on the rez - what could asphalt or concrete possibly say to that?

The blond from earlier stands at the corner passing out tracts on How To Be Saved. Another one from that morning joins her and they laugh at something then get compassionately serious when more students approach. No one is taking the tracts, or of the two who did, they take a quick look then drop them on the sidewalk. It's humiliating to see.

"I remember you from earlier. Thank you for the help," I say with my hand outstretched. The blond shakes my hand.

The man beside her reaches out shakes with an iron grip. The grip of white masculine supremacy. The grip of dominance. Another blond. Some conspiracy here or some kind of upside down world. Then Davis appears and joins the other two.

"Whoa. What the fuck. Oh, wait, that's why you wouldn't get high with us. So does this mean you're now born again into the everlasting? That why you found me? To save me?"

"We were worried about you, when we woke up and you were gone this morning. By the way what happened?"

"Short story, got attacked for being Native while hanging out with the spirit nation."

"Listen, you gotta come out to Zion with me," Davis says, speaking too loud, too quick, too giddy in his excitement. "I can't even describe it, you gotta come out there, see for yourself."

"What're you talking about? Zion?"

"Zion. It's a place out east of here, 40 acres mostly woods. We live communally. You can feel the love out there. It's like nothing I experienced before except the time with our company when our very lives depended on each of us being there for the other. You'd recognize it instantly, I did anyway. They built the whole place up from the ground by themselves. A bunch of freaks working together without fights and arguments. They, we get along because we're of one mind. I think you'd get it. I think you'd like it. Liam's our pastor, he's a strong spiritual leader. I think you'd get it."

"Why would I want to join you somewhere out in the woods? Pick up where I left off in some kind of Bravo Company only with some kind of religious Guru calling the shots? You been going around to the men in our company to save them, save us? Why would you want to do that?"

"I'd want to do that because you're fucked up out here, you're lost and you know it. I was lost but now I'm found. I have that circle around me again. You know what I mean. You know exactly what I mean. There's something absolutely familiar about it. How they live, how they function. Not exactly the same, no guns, no war but the same."

"Yeah, I know what you mean."

The others on the street corner are still handing out tracts, still ignored, still fools. People on the street call them Jesus freaks, consider them robotic and annoying for their inane comments. 'Have you ever heard of Jesus?' Who hasn't heard of Jesus. Like goddamned robots repeating the same thing over and over. But they were the only ones who had shown compassion, who didn't look away. They helped without question or judgement. Fuck.

Davis

❖

If it wasn't for Julian I wouldn't be here. If it wasn't for that moment in the war I wouldn't be here. If it wasn't for . . . . I owe my salvation to Jesus Christ my Lord and that is all. If it wasn't for that one moment in the jungle. My eyes opened then and I saw the whole of it, the entirety of it all in a flash. The whole eternity of it. Hell, that's what it was, hell, pure and simple the ghosts of all those farmers and their wives the ghosts of the children and their animals. The emptying of their fields the destruction of their lives. How were they to return to any semblance of family and home when their homes were burned to the ground? I am a new creature. I am forgiven all my sins. All my whoring, the shadow of my life is gone, disappeared. Thank you Jesus. If it wasn't for that one moment, seeing that slow motion grenade arcing toward Julian.

"Wait up," I call out when Julian walks off. "Come out to Zion, just see it, check it out. Have a meal, maybe hike out into the woods a ways. It's beautiful, you'll like it I'm sure. There are horses too, maybe we could take them out. Or maybe you could, I don't know horses the way you do."

"Horses?"

"Great horses, and lots of trails to venture out into. On the edge of BLM land, it goes on forever."

"Where's this place?"

"Out east, highway 72, keep going past Grey Willow to a little valley. Paved roads all the way. Well, until you get onto the land we call Zion. Aren't you even curious?"

"Yeah, actually I am curious but Jesus is your trip, not mine, okay?"

"Yeah, yeah, not a word from me about Jesus. Promise. So you'll come? I got Lee's car for the day. We can leave anytime. I'll buy you breakfast on the way."

"Pretty excited about this aren't you? A little too excited, maybe?"

"Yeah, yeah, nah, just glad to get back out there myself and want to show you what I'm up to. Show you my world. Not that it's any better than your world, just saying . . . . "

"Yeah, better shut up before you change my mind."

Julian

❖

A muddy one lane road leads past an army medic tent to a cluster of small cabins and a long building nestled in the trees. The mud road winds west bisecting a long narrow pasture with a small horse barn and some other small animal barns on one side and a mobile home on the other. The large, main building and cabins are bat and board painted green, lots of smoke coming out of little stovepipes. Paths made from wood chips lead from the cabins to the large building. Under the canopy of firs the whole of it is idyllic, something out of a child's fairy tale. Something childlike about the place, innocent, boy scout cute. Almost cuddly, tucked back in the woods. Long haired men and women in long skirts all leave the large building, line like, a column of ants. Scary.

Davis points to the big army mess tent, says that's where the sisters sleep.

"Even in this freeze?" I ask.

"Yeah, well yeah, I guess so. The sister's dorm won't be finished till Spring so for now they stay in there. It only got really cold that one time - last night."

"Really cold is an understatement. I was inside with you and that fire all night blazing and it was cold as shit."

Davis parks near the large metal building and we walk out toward the horse barn. A couple of horses, nice paints, watch our approach, the young one, curious, leans over the fence to be closer, follows us along the fence line. The older one is in foal, pretty far along but still ridable. She ignores us. From a trailer at the edge of the pasture a curtain closes. A woman inside watches us, hides her face behind sheer curtains. Between the trailers and the barns the mud road leads into the forest where it narrows: A forest that's been logged - a broken and weakened place. This land ails, I can feel it under my feet. Like land under cement it feels dead. Or dying. I want to ride up that trail, find out how far this sickness extends. How far the influence of these people has touched, infected, injured.

"Who do we talk to about taking the horses out?"

"Cass maybe, in the big trailer, or Lily. More likely Lily, she's the horse steward."

"The what?"

"Horse steward, she trains them, gives lessons, feeds, cleans you know - everything."

"Hmm."

The woman from the trailer has decided to join us at the barn. In her arms is a little one, maybe two years old, maybe less. She's native, full blood for sure, maybe Lakota.

"Ahó," she says as greeting. "I'm Cass, from Pine Ridge. You?"

"Julian, from Crow Creek, Dakota."

"Ahh, welcome to hell." Davis turns whiter than usual hearing these words from Cass. She looks at him and laughs. "Shocked? Ha, Liam knows how I feel. It's no secret. You like the horses? I can get Lily to saddle one up for you. She just got back from an unsuccessful mission to save a couple of Wasichus from themselves. Maybe you can do a better job of tracking and actually get them down off the mountain if they're not already frozen to the ground."

"Been out overnight? Why?"

"Following something, probably deer, maybe elk. My guess is they went up to hunt but without weapons it's a fool's errand."

"I'd like to ride out see what's ailing this land. I learned tracking from my uncles, guess I could help find the men."

A young woman in Levi's and cowboy boots comes out from the tack room and joins us.

"This is Lily, she's in charge of the horses," Cass says. I reach out my hand to shake hers, to introduce myself. She has kind eyes, soft red curls practically to her waist. Lean, tough, strong but at the same time insecure or disconnected. She makes no eye contact, looks down, seems anxious to get this over with. Whatever this is.

"Julian wants to go out with the horses, help with the search."

"I followed the tracks as far as the ridge. It's solid granite above the tree line and steep down the other side. I could see the trail but couldn't get Maggie to go down to it. She'd probably follow Vienna though. You know horses?"

"I know horses," I say.

"I'll saddle up Vienna. You can ride her around a bit, get used to her while I tack up Maggie."

Vienna is a good responsive mare. Soft sides and mouth, easy to ride, generous horse. "Nice gal you have here," I say when Lily joins me. "You train her?"

"She's older but I worked with her since she's been here to get her more responsive. I'm teaching some of the elders to ride. You moving out here?"

"Not me, just visiting. An old friend convinced me I should come out and see the place. Something's wrong here, do you feel it? In the land, I feel it coming from the land."

"No . . . I'm from LA so not sure I'd be able to tell if the land was wrong. I'm just glad to be here and taking care of the horses."

The churned up part of the trail leads off from the main road not far from where the canopy darkens the woods. Still the feeling of hollow deadness remains. We follow the trail a long ways up a gentle rise then something shifts.

"You feel that?

"Feel what?"

"Something in the land. It shifted, right back there."

"I didn't feel anything."

I stop and turn around. "We have to go back, just a short ways, I want you to feel it. Just follow me back. Close your eyes and feel. Follow me back down toward the barns. Don't think, just feel. And don't open your eyes."

I close my eyes too, to get a better sense of what I'm feeling. Sitting there on Vienna with my eyes closed I feel a softening in my chest and then as I urge her back toward the barns there is a shift again, a hollowness, nothing. With eyes open the environment looks the same. Same trees same underbrush but the land changes.

"I felt something. Something changed right there. What is that?" Lily asks.

"Okay, turn back and do it in the other direction, eyes closed again."

"Yes, yes, I felt it again only this way, coming away from Zion it's like breathing. It's not me though. What is it?"

"Where are we?" I ask.

Lily looks into the forest, for a long time just looking. "There," she says finally. "There, right there, you can see where the BLM fence line runs. And on the far side down below, it starts up again. It's old and broken down but if it continued it would cross the trail right here where this thing is. This change. What is that?"

"I know what it is. I know exactly what it is. Up here it's the land breathing out her spirit, alive and resonant to our spirit, same to same. And back on the other side, down there, I point back toward Zion and the cabins and the barns. "Back there, nothing. Something's wrong, the land is hurt, shunned maybe into withdrawal." Lily just stares back down the trail, says nothing.

We walk in silence after that. Lily saying nothing more than what's needed to guide us. Then all at once she can't stop talking.

She's trying to unfeel what she's feeling? She's up ahead and I don't say anything back and soon I realize she's not talking to me, not really, she's talking to herself trying to back herself out, to put herself back together again in the fashion of what she's trying so hard to be.

Lily's tension courses through Maggie's sensitive back, sides and mouth. Agitated and prancing Maggie refuses to go forward and starts backing up, buckling up on her haunches, preparing to spin. I catch up to Maggie, dismount, stroke Vienna's face then Maggie's and talk quietly about hay and pastures and irritating two leggeds then mount back up and walk ahead. Maggie follows quietly.

"She just needs a leader for a few minutes, that's all. I don't know the way so I'll just slow up here in a minute and you pass me."

The ridge at the top is as she described. I dismount, stand near the edge. I take out my medicine pouch, offer tobacco and a song to the eagle nation. An eagle approaches from the west, glides overhead, circling on a current of air directly above us. It calls back once before heading down the canyon toward the north. I call back a greeting and a farewell, "mitakuyas." Below, a ribbon of water shimmers in the bright sun.

"Who are you? What was that?"

"I'm Julian."

"No, that's not my question."

"I offered tobacco and prayed to the wingeds, made relations with the winged nation, so this one came by to say hi. I know them and they know me. Maybe it's because I'm Native or maybe it's just because I'm paying attention. That's where we need to go," I say, pointing to the trail below.

"Okay. It's just I've never seen anything, felt anything, like this before. I feel the land like it's inside me instead of some kind of blank nothing, like physical objects - cement or a wall - out there. I'm not making any sense."

"Yeah, you make sense, you make perfect sense. It's just you never felt it before. Now you have you'll miss it because you know the difference. It's strong on the rez, that's why I know it so well. Mostly off the rez it's all deadened. This BLM land is not for some reason."

"But the eagle."

"Animals know."

"Know what?"

"Know us. Sense us. They connect with what is connected, what is familiar. That's all, nothing special."

"Nothing special?" she says laughing.

"No, it's natural - nature - and we're nature too if you think of it. But where are we?"

"The trail's visible from here," she says, standing off to the side, pointing down a steep granite grade. "This is where I gave up. No way could I get Maggie to go down there. No way I wanted her to go actually."

"We can do this. She'll follow Vienna. I'm okay with this, Vienna will pick up on that. You just need to relax. Breathe, just focus on that. Breathe. Follow for just this stretch."

The horses walk down the side of the mountain to the trail without hesitating. Maggie head to tail with Vienna. Lily has her eyes closed but she's breathing soft and steady. Trust.

"We're at the trail now, you can open your eyes."

The trail is narrow with low hanging branches. Most are broken and loosely hanging from the elk crashing through earlier and easy to pass through but with a lot of scraping, scratching and ducking. Deer don't need height and on their trails the trees and brush are lower to the ground compared to what two leggeds or elk would prefer. This is where the herd slowed down.

After a half hour or so I dismount. I need to be closer to the ground to see. Lily dismounts as well and we walk in silence. The forest here is broken in spots, too many thrashed bushes. The elk must have spread out seeking easier passage or even settled down and returned to grazing behavior, no longer following a single file trail. It's hard but not impossible to find an occasional boot print from one of the men. And among the branches the occasional spot of blood. We follow the trail with the bootprints and soon it becomes obvious we are also following the blood.

"You see the blood there?" I ask.

"No, show me."

"There, on the blackberry leaves and there, on that rock. The boots go this way too, have you seen them?"

"I saw them back there when we turned off the main trail. That's when the elk tracks changed."

"The men are following a wounded one," I say. "Or one of the men is wounded. Either way we're getting closer to them. You smell the smoke?" Lily stops and breathes deeply. "They're a long way off if that smoke's theirs. And I believe it's theirs. They might be sending up smoke for a signal to whoever might be looking for them. That's smart anyway."

"You think it was a bad idea for them to run off after the herd to begin with?"

"I think they got ahead of themselves. Typical Wasichu."

"Wasichu?"

"Eaters of the fat. Wasichu, what we call the white man. They take the best for themself. No offense. Not all white people."

The trail generally aims toward the smoke. As we approach, the trail narrows and eventually we are walking over ferns and downed logs. No more than a few prints, elk and human, to lead us but the smoke is undeniable here. The horses balk, unwilling to get too close to fire.

"I can go on alone," Lily says. "You stay with the horses?"

"If they need help getting out or bringing the meat out, I'm better equipped to help. You'd just have to come back and get me." Lily looks beyond the visible trail, nods, takes Vienna's reins.

Tracks show the men were less certain or maybe tired. One man left the trail, stood for a while. The tracks beyond are muddied like they'd been walking back and forth. Tracking on foot for game, for the injured, not stalking the enemy. No scope, no smell of death or the soft moaning sounds of the dying. Just this easy narrow deer trail. And silence. Too quiet, suddenly too quiet. Tandem breathing suddenly and I know I'm the one being tracked.

"I'm here with Lily and the horses." I call out. "From down below, a place called Zion. Looking for a couple of men, hunters, maybe they have an elk they need help with?"

Silence. Then in the background of awareness, movement. And then soft rustling and a man emerges from the stand of firs up ahead. His clothes are covered in blood and pieces of flesh, his beard has flecks of blood and what looks like raw meat around his mouth. His hair is stringy, oily, pasted to his head in places. He has a wild untethered look in his eyes and is holding his knife out.

His voice direct but flat, "What do you want?"

"Like I said I'm here with Lily. You come up here from Zion?"

"Yeah."

"You need help bringing anything down?" Feels like I'm dealing with a madman, unpredictable and liable to strike. "Like an elk? I'm Julian, just visiting, came up to help Lily track, help find you guys."

"Don't need your help. We got here on our own and can get back on our own."

"Anyone'd need help with a large animal. You are the elk hunter aren't you?"

"Yeah, I'm that."

"Okay then, let's see what we have to work with. You want to show me where that elk is?"

"Can't do that."

"Oookay. You want to come down with us? Get you down off this mountain and into a warm cabin or wherever you're staying down there."

"Can't do that."

"What can you do then? Just tell me what you need."

"What I need is for you to leave me alone. I don't know you. You Born Again? You in the Ministry?"

"No, just visiting. Here with Davis. You know Davis?"

"Haven't met Davis but there's plenty brothers I don't know."

"So . . . ?"

"So nothing, I said leave me alone. Jesus sent me up here to do His work and to take care of the people, like Moses, to bring down mana out of the wilderness and feed the people. But you know what?" He looks back up the trail from where he came, turns and walks off. "I don't need no help. I can serve my Lord here, on my own, just like that. Don't need nobody, Do I Jesus?" His voice trails off as he ambles up the trail. Fuck this.

Lily's already on Maggie's back. "I heard Sawyer. He sounds strange even for Sawyer. We need to get back down to Zion. Tell Liam."

"What we need to do is figure out a better way to get here, a road, or something you can drive a truck on, otherwise anyone else, someone from your group'll be no better off than we are trying to get him down. That guy is nuts. Let's ride back up the trail and get a better view. We're still a ways from the bottom, from the lower creek. We might need to ride all the way down, find a way to the creek and then up from there."

"Thank you, I know you didn't sign up for this. He wasn't like that when he left."

Lily is walking ahead as we make our way around the area Sawyer was heading. A circuitous path with Sawyer at the center. Lily rides intuitively, barely moves and her horse knows what she wants of her. Same way my horse responds to me. Easy, responsive, open, unafraid.

"How is it you ended up here? This place is beautiful, familiar somehow, but for the religion part."

"Yeah, sometimes I wonder what it would feel like to just be here. Enjoy the place. There's hardly any time to do that. Summers I work 18 hours a day with the horses and lessons and I make bread for lunches and dinner. We only just got Sundays off about a month ago. The sisters, that is. The brothers always had Sundays off, I guess they didn't notice we had no days off. I'm sorry, I shouldn't have spoken that way. I'm just tired, I think. It's easier being busy to be honest. I do miss writing though, there's no time for that, or reading except for the Bible."

"Were you brought up Christian?"

"No, and I'd never even been to church before I came to the Lord and joined the ministry. Now I'm just grateful I was chosen," Lily says.

"Grateful? Hmm, I guess I've not learned that quality. I could say I'm grateful to be alive, grateful nobody died today. Low standards, I guess. And Chosen? Hmm, I don't even know what that means. It's possible Marty is dead, though. Did you think of that?"

"I did. I didn't see Sawyer but I heard him and the way he was talking to you made me think he was hiding something. It froze last night. A really deep freeze . . . . Where were you last night?"

"Illyria. Inside by a warm fire. Feeling good, until the old men. Then I was just cold."

"Old men?"

"I took a walk early and some grumpy old white guys wanted me off their reservation. But then some of your friends helped me out. That was how I started my day and now I'm here."

"It was God. God called you here."

"I'd like to think it was the generosity of strangers acting from the kindness of their heart . . . . I don't really want to get into a theological debate here, you okay with that?"

"Yeah, okay. Only it's hard not to. I've been out here so long with just the brethren that I hardly know how to have normal conversations anymore. Sorry, that's the second confession I should have kept to myself."

"Don't need to apologize. I think you've kept to yourself, kept to the horses, separated yourself, to save yourself from annihilation, from annihilating your Self. It's a shame you'd have to do that."

"What? how do you get that?"

"Your connection to the horses is the opposite of your connection to the two leggeds. Shows in your face, your body, what you don't say. You're in tune with the horses, know how to feel your way into and through their fears and reactions to what confronts them. But you, you seem cut off - a cut-out version of a person playing a part. Reacting how you're supposed to react, feeling what you're supposed to feel. For instance, what was it like when you woke up in the tent, freezing. Did you even feel it. Or is that sin?"

"How'd you know I woke up in the tent freezing. I never mentioned that."

"It was something Davis mentioned. About how all you 'sisters' bunk in a tent while most of the 'brothers live in a dorm."

Lily is quiet for a long time.

Something about grateful, happy people I don't trust and I don't like. Nobody who is honest can be that flatlined. So I needle and jab like this, probably a need to know someone else hurts too. I hurt so you hurt. If that's all this is then who's being dishonest? And when she does finally speak up it's not about grateful anymore.

"I did wake up totally confused and without any way to understand why. Something. Something I didn't know. I've never felt like that before. Like something life threatening happened but I didn't know it or what it was. I didn't even realize I was cold until someone said it had dropped to 30 below. Then when Liam came in from the trailer I was angry. I thought he was a hypocrite. Those were feelings I shut out before they could take root, words I couldn't hear, even inside my own head - until now. Those words, those feelings, how is it possible to shut off something like that so I didn't even know? Ahh, shouldn't have spoken."

"Shut off from yourself? So who's in charge? Is it Liam? Hey, I'm not criticizing. I was in Nam and someone was always in charge, I was responsible for learning to shoot and for following orders. And you know what? I fucking miss it. That's my reality, that's my confession. I got used to the narrowness of that life and I got used to someone else being the responsible party. Children get to live that way, we're supposed to grow up though and I hate it. I fucking hate it."

"God is our Father His word guides us, not Liam. God has just given Liam wisdom in the Word and a special relationship with Him. We listen to God in our hearts."

"You can hear God but you can't hear yourself. How's that work?"

"Reading the Bible I know what's of God. Without the word I'm in danger of being beguiled by the Devil. God wants to be our Father, he wants to give us peace. It's the only way we can have peace." But Lily's voice is flat. There's no conviction.

"Like I said I hate being an adult and responsible for every damned thing all of a sudden, but I don't want to stay a child forever. Or find a place that will support my desire to stay a child and not take responsibility for my time here. Birth is painful, but you can't live in the womb forever. Anyway n'dn way is different, Jesus was a warrior and like the buffalo nation he sacrificed himself so the people might live. He's my brother in ceremony. I know him well but not the way you think of as knowing him."

The trail finally branches off. Below us a road swings into view. A narrow dirt road, a logging road perhaps. "You think this way might lead us back to Zion?"

"It has to tie into some main road," Lily says. "I think we should follow it to the right."

Lily leads us to where the trail and road meet. The creek is still some ways down in the valley but the trees have thinned out and it feels like we're coming into some kind of neighborhood.

We ride in silence.

Wade

❖

"You men get that truck and take it out on the dirt road behind the creek and out beyond it onto the BLM land and look for Sawyer and Marty," Liam says. "Lily's out on horseback so keep an eye out for her too. She might have seen signs of where they are."

The dirt road is slick, still covered in black ice here and there and the tires are too bald for travel away from Zion and that's usually not a problem but this black ice has me worried. Brothers in the truck bed look out at the land, search through the trees and into peoples' yards. We're still too close to our road to expect to see anything but we look anyway. Serious and quiet. A day off, it's what I asked for was a day off and now this. Driving around the back roads looking into peoples' windows. Sunday driving, or cruising, feels like the old days on Colorado Boulevard, ha. Hunched down, driving slow so as not to lose anyone out the back of the truck. Pretending for just a minute. *Jesus, find those guys for us, lead us to them.* Or not, it feels good to just drive.

"There, stop the truck!" Paul beside me in the cab points to a trail that leads up the hill into BLM land. The brothers all pile out of the bed and hike up the trail. There's no sign of the missing brothers but it's a trail so we follow it up the hillside. After about a quarter mile we come to a ridge that provides a good view. Above the tree line the sun on the frosted forest glistens and the icy breeze hits us in the face. Charlie sits to take in the view then the others sit.

"Anyone see anything?"

"A lot of forest out there. Illyria's that way," Charlie points west. "Wonder if they just hitched to town? Not the first time that's happened. Most go in the middle of the night though. Marked after and backslid. I saw Mitch in town last week. You remember, he left in the night a couple of months ago? I crossed the street to avoid him. He saw me, waved, started to follow me across the street then figured it out that I was avoiding him. The look on his face? Like he didn't expect it. Kind of made me sorry but I had to do it. If you reject our Lord then that's like stabbing Jesus in the back, isn't it? Or stabbing us in the back?"

"Anyone see anything," I repeat.

"This is Christ's Ridge," Andrew stands up prophet-like and proclaims in his most solemn voice. "The Lord has provided us with a vision. As He provided for the Children of Israel - a pillar of fire in the darkness and in the daytime a pillar of smoke. See there? A pillar. Of. Smoke."

Off to the south a thin wisp of smoke rises up out of the trees. Barely visible but it's definitely smoke. The brothers scramble down the trail and back into the truck. As the road narrows it becomes more deeply rutted and after another few miles it dead ends in a wide turn around. BLM land is a web of signless logging roads that dead end. Beyond the road is a deeply rutted forest trail the loggers use to bring the logs out, this one won't support a vehicle. At least not our vehicle. Without an overhead view we are rats in a maze. Damn.

"Anybody smell smoke?" Paul asks.

The brothers get real still and sniff the air.

"There were a couple other side roads back there, we just

need to turn around and take one," Paul says. "All we need is to get deeper into the forest and drop down again to where the creek flows. That smoke came from down in the canyon, nearer the creek."

"We are assuming the smoke is coming from Sawyer and Marty. It's possible someone's using a wood stove," I say.

"Where's your faith?" Andrew scolds. "God sent us a sign. The Children of Israel were turned back from the promised land for lack of faith and made to wander for 40 years in the wilderness - for refusing to trust Him and submit to Him." Andrew is adamant.

Lily

❖

The neighborhood comes into sight as we turn the sharp corner of the logging road and step up onto the graded street - a shock after being submerged in the forest. Images of Disneyland hit me; perfectly ordered rows of pastel houses, tightly squared and angled bushes, evenly spaced rocks lined up designating walkways and driveways. Behind is a forest, cut and scarred in places, bleeding and torn in others but still she holds her own. Here, she's given up. Julian has infected me. I'm hit by the emptiness here. The clinching tightness in the chest. The lack of air. Her response to what? to us? to people? Be fruitful and multiply, and replenish the earth, and subdue it: *and have dominion over the fish of the sea, and over the foul of the air, and over every living thing that moveth upon the face of earth.* Subdue it. That's what we've done and that's how I know who I am. Subdue it. Subdue. It. I am subdued, the earth is subdued. God is our Father and he guides into righteousness even as we walk in sin - subdued. The earth is crushed here. But that place, that breathing place is not crushed, not even with all the efforts to take from her and abuse her generosity. And I realize that I've always felt like I was in a park. An environment created by people. Even here, thinking someone makes these narrow little trails, someone checks on them, clears out the downed branches. Replaces some invisible light bulbs. And now I can't unfeel it - the reality of the actual breathing earth. Julian has infected me. This breathing open expression of what? Spirit? This opening of the lungs; is it the land that breathes or is it just me imagining? Sweet grace or nothing. Nothing. Nothing. An oak growing into an oak, simple and pure. Not a bush. *You must be a bush if you want to be loved by me.* I don't want to be a bush. I was born from the seed of an oak. Who talks like that? Who makes up the kind of stories that force a tree, an oak, an ancient spreading oak or a cottonwood to stunt itself. To change its nature to be a bush.

Julian in silence rides up ahead on Vienna. He rides like he's been on horses all his life. Like he knows the nature of horses and he knows me. Knows my horse dreams. Do you? Have horse dreams? Julian? Do you know the back of a horse and the flaming ears that lead you into the final stretch of the mountain trail, the one that leads to the very top of the mountain? Does your horse emerge from the sea, frothing and storming forward like a torrent of rain and hail but held between the legs gently, ever so gently and with reins held in soft fingers. Fingers that know the very mind of you. That know the back and the heart of what it means to know a horse. And what, and what . . .

"I used to write poetry," I say. Julian turns in the saddle, startled by my unexpected words. "I haven't written any poetry since I came to the Lord."

"Why's that?"

"It was how I understood my world, myself too."

"Why'd you stop then?"

Subdued. Subdue. It. And have dominion over every living thing that moveth upon the earth. "You think it's possible to kill yourself without dying? Kill but not the body?"

Julian halts Vienna and waits for me to catch up.

"Yeah, people do it all the time. People work really hard at it. For some, life on the rez is like a single minded pursuit of exactly that. The war was that for me. I wanted to kill. I refused to believe it was me I was trying so hard to kill, but it was. Suicide of the soul. But I don't believe we can actually kill the soul, if that's what you mean."

"Poetry kept me. And I haven't even mourned losing it. Feels like a black tarry substance growing inside me now though. That neglected part that I have to ask forgiveness for."

"Your soul."

"You think I'm trying to kill my soul?"

"You know you brought this up, and to be honest, yes. That's what I think and I believe that's what you think, deep down."

"You infected me when you made me feel the earth. And now here in this neighborhood she's dead again."

"Yeah, I felt it too, just back there. Mitakuyas."

"Yes. What?"

"Mitakuye Oyasin - it means all my relations. It's a way of acknowledging we are all related, not just the two leggeds but also the green and growing, the forest. It's what you're feeling or now what you're not feeling. That connection. It's the ancient way of being, it's Indian way of being but not just n'dns. Maybe there's hope for you. Down deep I think you know you didn't come here to save your soul, you came here to kill who you are. Maybe you're guilty about something. Poetry is voice. Kill your voice, kill your soul. The expression of your being."

Someone inside me is laughing. Mocking laughter at my choice to be here, *you knew it all along. You knew what you were up to.* Then away and more laughter. There, floating in the air above and over the vast canyon he glides. Sing-song voice like a child's rhyme, *you knew it all along and yet here you stay.* Maggie beneath me canters easily on the flat, level surface and I drive her forward with my seat, move with her as though joined. Behind me Julian calls out something but I can't understand the words, the voice inside is too loud. The voice that calls my name and laughs, telling me to Wake Up. Inside me is a black tarry substance, a lake of it, and it is my companion. *Cast out the demon,* I hear. That's what they'll say. *Demon possession. Return to the fold,* they'll say. *A lamb to the slaughter,* I'll call out. Run, Maggie run, we two.

Like in my dream again, we are running and flying, this time Maggie's ears aflame. My ears burning. I want to run forever but up ahead in the distance I see a truck, the truck from Zion. It's so tiny, so insignificant from this distance. How could it have such power over me? Yet it does and as I approach, the brothers in the truck bed wave and I stop, snapped back in an instant into the good girl of the scriptures, the one I've become, the switch I have no control over? This is not what I wanted to find. Constriction in my chest, a thin cord, a piano string wrapped around my ribs. If I break it the music will die, if I don't it will crush me.

Andrew

❖

And the children of God were led that day by the pillar of smoke. Just as the children of Israel were led through the desert for those forty years. And they did cry out against the Lord God of Hosts and complain with great murmurings. So great was their sin that they blamed God for their pain and suffering. So great was their sin that they hardened their hearts.

But the Lord that day rewarded His servant Andrew for his faith and did bring forth from the wilderness an helpmeet. Even the woman, Lily, who He had chosen for His servant on that day. And I say unto you, my servant Andrew, that I will give unto you the woman you have chosen, the woman Lily. And you will comfort her in all the days of her vanity.

Wade

❖

"It's Lily, Praise the Lord, it's Lily," Andrew stands, yells from the back of the truck and bangs on the roof for me to stop. Behind us and visible in the rear view mirror is Lily coming around a bend, riding up on the truck.

"Have you seen Marty and Sawyer?" one of the brothers calls out. "We've been driving around and looking for the way to get closer to that smoke. See it there? We have an idea that they might be signaling us." The truck stops and the guys jump down.

Lily stops at a distance and calls out, "You're right he's at the fire. Not sure he's signaling though. He's pretty spaced out, maybe from the freeze last night, kind of out of his mind actually. Not sure what happened during the night - if they were able to get out of the cold. We didn't see Marty, though. We were looking for a trail that would lead up to them from this side. We came up on Sawyer from the other side, from the trail they followed down from the ridge." Lily points up the mountain in the direction they rode down from.

Andrew stands up in the bed of the truck and calls back to her, "We? Who's with you?"

"Julian, he came out with Davis, he's helping me track them."

"You're not supposed to be alone with a man without a chaperone. You know that. Is he even born again? Who is he?"

Julian appears from around the bend, stops beside Lily, listens to the talk, nods, acknowledging me. Apparently the word chaperone is all he heard. "You need a chaperone?" He says, laughing. "Wouldn't have imagined that. No, *couldn't* have imagined that."

"Andrew, this is not helpful. Right now we need to find the brothers. Especially since something might be wrong. Lily," I call out, "do you think you can get us close enough to hike the rest of the way?

"We can try. They're up half a mile maybe less. We would need to find a trail or make a trail. Honestly, though he's kind of scary, Sawyer is. Julian came up almost to his camp and Sawyer stood him off with a knife. A big knife. And wouldn't talk about Marty when he asked. Oh, and he's covered in blood and stuff."

Lily and Julian ride ahead, lead us down the dirt road. The neighborhood road borders BLM land and sits at the base of the mountains. Beyond and to the East and South is endless forest. A spire of smoke rises above the treetops in the clear blue sky.

The truck fills the canyon with the stink of diesel and with the voices of men. Excited voices, on the verge of discovery voices, punctuated by the occasional Amen or Praise the Lord. Glad to be out in the sun and out of the mud voices.

I feel myself walking with Lily and Julian. Feel something like embarrassment for the men in the truck, for myself. Feel myself up there, on the trail with those two on the back of a horse. Forgive me Lord.

Andrew

❖

And the word of the Lord came unto him who could hear. That woman Jezebel will be punished unless you redeem her for she is the daughter of Eve who caused Adam to eat of the tree of good and evil and so was turned out from the garden that I prepared for them.

And who is this Jezebel my Lord, of whom do you speak?

Be still and know that I am God. That woman Lily has turned her back on me in my own house, upon this land that I have given even unto you. Know her by her name. Her name is Jezabel.

But you have given her unto me to be my helpmate.

And it is for you to save her from the hour of her sin. Take her even as David took Bathsheba and make her your wife. Only then will she find her True Salvation.

Lily

❖

They laugh and talk and pray and sing. The songs of our worship. Always songs of heaven, our next home. Or songs of unity among the brethren. So many of the brothers and sisters write songs, write praises to our Lord. The music pours out of them. So it's just me that can't do it. I have no real talent for praise apparently. My poems tended toward the morose my cousin used to say. In my adamant objection I gave myself away. "Thou doth protest too much," she parried.

Have I made a huge mistake I can't unmake? The sensation of salt, the craving for salt, fills my body with something, something, what? Longing? Expectation? Nighttime? The taste of sin? Deep abiding hunger? Salt intensifies taste. Salt generates thirst. Has this ever present craving for salt made my body the one in charge of speaking what I won't, what I can't admit? That my righteous proclamations of absolute fulfillment through Christ are a sham, that I am saltstarved and craving something elemental. In the body, in the soul? Have I made a huge mistake?

Julian rides up ahead, shaking his head, laughing? Disdain

bleeds from his body but he tries to hide it. Laughing at us, at me? I want to hate him for it but I can't because I feel it myself. That's what it is. And why did I chose to commit my life to these ways, to this Christ, to this place, to Liam? Because I believed I had a vision, a moment that couldn't be undone even when I tried. Then there's Hell. So I have to save people from Hell. I have to save myself from Hell. That's why I'm still here. But before, before the part about Hell, what was it? Something about God's actual hand writing the scriptures in the sky? Or was it because being on the road had lost its magic and I was alone squatting in an old abandoned building, panhandling for breakfast and dinner with no way out?

This man beside me speaks his mind without reworking it to fit with something outside himself. Looks at the men in the truck and laughs. Who ever heard of chaperones? Who goes along with this foolishness. I'm not supposed to be here. I can't unthink that. And I can't unthink Hell.

"You're crying, I'm sorry. Did I do that to you?" Julian slows to close the gap between us and speaks just above a whisper.

But I can't answer. Words are impossible. I know, I've learned to know, that to speak is sin. "There is a trail that starts here," I call out in my clearest voice to the brothers behind us in the truck. "I believe it will lead you to where that smoke is. To Sawyer and Marty." I point up the hillside to a trail that becomes visible just above the road. It's a well worn trail maybe it will get them there. Maybe it won't.

"We're going to ride back now," I call out before they get too close. Before they can say anything.

Charlie

❖

The trail starts just above a rocky outcropping that borders the edge of the road, we scramble over it and begin the hike towards the men. Paul calls for quiet as a way of stealth so as not to spook Sawyer with our numbers and in case he's as deranged as Lily implied. It's easy to follow this band of merry men up through the hills and search for one of our own. Maybe this is all I needed, this walk, this silence, these woods. Sawyer is a man of the woods more than any of us, yet here we are, thinking we're going to rescue him.

The trail up the hill is steep then veers sideways, a soft deer trail that is narrow and low slung with branches. The going gets easier as we rise in elevation and enter more open forest, and leave behind the brush growing nearer the road. Here the trail widens and opens up to vistas of the valleys all around us. Sparkling green vistas of seemingly endless forest and above us a granite ridge - Eagles Nest.

Paul stops the men with a fist in the air. In the silence we hear a voice. A distant faint sound but the cadence is definitely a human voice. "Can't you men walk silently?" He quietly scolds. None of us knows how to walk silently over twigs and branches but we try and in fact actually move much more quietly. Enough so that the voice remains audible as we go.

Clearly it is Sawyer's voice but too rhythmic to be conversation, prayer perhaps? The smoke is visible only at certain times and often we move in the opposite direction but soon the camp comes into view. Paul steps into the clearing first then several of the others. Sawyer doesn't look up, just continues speaking in the low rhythmic voice we heard before, a prayer.

There is a large gutted carcass plus pieces of odd meat scattered at a distance around the small fire. It smells bad here, not death bad but funky butcher shop bad. We instinctively move up close to the fire, circling around Sawyer.

"I was about to start cutting this elk up into pieces so we could drag 'em out over the mountain limb by limb." Sawyer speaks so quietly it seems almost to himself. "A lot of help y'all are after I came all this way to provide. The Lord guided me and then I had to wait all night in the cold. You know how cold it was last night? Cold enough to have to get right up inside this here elk. Wasn't for this kill I'd be frozen hard to the ground. Frozen hard to the ground."

"Good to see you too," Paul scolds.

"Where's Marty?" Andrew asks.

Sawyer is oblivious. "We better get cutting then. Any you brought a knife or a saw or anything?"

"Where's Marty?" Paul asks, finally disturbed at the carnage in front of us.

"Not here obviously. Don't ask me, I'm not his keeper."

Something is wrong here, seriously way beyond wrong but I keep my mouth shut. Wade steps forward about to assert some authority, rebuke Sawyer maybe but then Marty shows up – comes out from behind a stand of trees, pieces of flesh and dried blood on his jacket.

"Marty," Paul calls out, "we thought . . . where have you been? We were all worried when we didn't see you."

Marty looks back at Sawyer, shrugs, I've been here, gathering firewood and whatever. What'd you think? You see this beauty? She'll provide us with meat through the winter. The Lord has provided for us like He did for the Children of Israel."

Marty stands proud over the elk, smiling over at Sawyer. A real bond between them.

"Between us we can carry it whole to the truck, it's just down the trail - straight down," Paul says.

Sawyer ignores Paul, our elder, anointed by God. Sargentlike Paul tries to take control of the situation but Sawyer is wily up here in his element and even Paul is unable face him down. Sawyer, who's probably twenty-three to Paul's nineteen and who isn't just backwoods wise but streetwise has always run Paul in circles.

"Any you brought a knife or a saw? Cutting this thing up smaller would make a big difference bringing her back down to Zion."

"No, and it's just us. The truck's just a short hike down the hill though, then we can drive it back."

"We'll lose meat if we can't keep her off the ground. I'll quarter her, use my knife then we can carry instead of drag. First we got to skin her, though. Easier while she's whole. Paul, you and the others hold the hind legs and me and Marty and Charlie will pull off the skin."

Sawyer cuts around the hocks and loosens the skin with his knife as the skin and hide separate. The men sit on the ground and hold on like a tug of war with the elk between.

"It would have been easier if we'd done it last night but we needed the extra protection of her hide to get us through the night." Marty says.

The skin comes off slow and with resistance. Even in the frigid cold we're all sweating but the work of it feels good. Just doing it. Without the layers of God and righteousness and laying up treasures in heaven.

"Okay, let's cut 'er up boys," Sawyer says once the hide's been pulled off. "Marty, you help me here by stretching out the hind leg and Wade you take the other one. Pull hard and hold."

The knife slices through flesh and grinds through the cartilage around joints. Sawyer moves quickly while the brothers watch, transfixed. Among the obvious body parts other pieces of meat and bone are scattered about the camp. The hide is separate and the head. Huge head.

"I'll drive the truck back, get the chain saw and then we can get this done. We'll be here all day with this knife," Paul says.

"Forget that," Sawyer says without looking up or even slowing his work. "You guys just take down the parts that'er done. The head and hide too. They're lighter now and you can at least help by carrying," he says to Paul.

Andrew and Wade hike down one of the hindquarters. Hauling it between them to the truck.

Just beyond the ring of the fire pit is a long bone and a slab of meat. Sawyer's sweating, digging deep into the spine, mumbling incoherent until I pick up the long bone, then he gets very still, very intense.

"Don't touch that. Don't touch that I said."

"Why not? What's this from?"

"Young wolf. Come up on us and we had to sacrifice him."

"I don't see any fur."

"What the fuck do you know about survival? Wolves and coyotes come 'cause of the smell, this one come up first. Had to scatter him around the camp so the others in the pack would keep away. I don't know what they did with the rest of their brother but he kept them out."

Lily

❖

We ride back along the road the way we came but instead of continuing on toward Zion I turn up a side trail that I hadn't noticed before. I have no idea where I'm going or why but for this irresistible urge. The trail leads us up a steep incline and as we make some progress toward the tree line it begins to feel familiar. Familiar in an odd way, not familiar like I've been here before, rather some inner flash or charge, déjà vu? Then the land opens up and we are above the tree line and I know where we are. There, near the ledge is the tree from my dream, Tony's tree. I dismount and lead Maggie to it, tying the reins up to a thin branch. Julian watches silently from Vienna's back, he makes no move to join me. He is a respectful man and for some reason just this small gesture brings back the tears.

At the ledge, leaning over, I press my palms into the sharp granite surface. The dream returns in flashes. The crows, the man flying above, the sound of the river below, Karl speaking in rhyme, the flying man's song, 'Free fall flow river flow on and on it goes . . . sing underwater 'till the end, 'till the bitter end.' Till the bitter end? That's not how the song goes. But that's how the dream song goes. The glowing quality of this place intensifies the canyon and the tree tops. Numinous. Like glittering knife edges, sharp and ominous pointing to the sky, tempting until I draw back, control this deadly urge to fling myself over the edge.

Julian stands watch by the tree beside Maggie, sitting on Vienna, a sentinel. Without speaking I mount Maggie and we start back down the trail. Silence and the thoughts swirling bring on the real truth: That I feel more honest beside this stranger and that he feels more human than these others, these saved ones. The brethren, the fellowship of the saints, the chosen of God, the elect, the set-apart and the only ones in possession of truth. Truth. Except that they, we, are so very lacking in human qualities, so calculated in all our talk of love. Or maybe it's just me.

Back on the trail the long stretching vista of existential dread returns from the days before my conversion. The vision in my head of the future, my future as an adult. The rock, pushing the rock up the hill only to watch it roll back down, over and over; eternal labor, Sisyphus' scream into the empty air and nothing more than the routine of the day to comfort - the evening drink and the news and and . . . Julian's presence like a mirror reflects back my hidden fears, hidden doubts but hidden from who, myself? if not myself then who? God? My sisters in the faith? My brothers? What if I spoke, what if I really asked the questions? Then I would be responsible for planting seeds of doubt in someone's heart, and there's the rub, I would be responsible for them. My voice, my spoken words responsible for all eternity - their everlasting sojourn in Hell everlasting, everlasting. But Julian knows something without words. He knows and rides on, quietly on Vienna, the solid, safe, silently listening mare. Outside this place. How? How is it possible for someone to be outside the argument of God - a strong oak on his own growing into fullness without need of salvation outside this whole spiritual dimension of good and evil heaven and Hell in sin or forgiven. How is that possible? Fearstates and my hands shake it is the cold. It is not the cold. Breathe breathe These thoughts are pure and crystal clear and I am afraid yet not afraid.

Not afraid. How is that possible? Behind me I hear laughter. Same laughter as my dream. *Don't take yourself so seriously,* he says. *You are not God.*

Twisting in the saddle but behind me Julian is not there. The trail is long and straight and has been for some time. I am alone. Maggie jumps at a covey of quail, jumps sideways, almost unseating me. She quickly settles down as I consciously relax - go slack in my muscles, pretend calm, project safety, fake it, stop, wait for Vienna. Wait for Julian. Fake it.

Julian

❖

What's scarier than war? Scarier than being shot at with live rounds, having grenades lobbed in your direction, seeing friends break and shatter? What's scarier than being in the midst of a place that believes it's okay to kill people. That gives everyone permission to go out and kill people, that gives medals for killing people? This place. *This* place is scarier. Scary as shit. A familiar mind fuck, give me your mind and I will make of you a soldier, a killing machine a part of the whole for the sake of the country. This place wants more. Give me your soul. Keep nothing for yourself. Body, mind, soul and spirit, forever, not just a four year stint; isn't that the spiel? Scary as shit. Get me the hell out of here.

Lily hasn't said anything for a long time, not since I caught up to her. Since the truck caught up to us, since she abruptly left them on their own when I thought we were helping track, since then, she's closed down. These are her people. Her total world. The isolation out here is complete. They don't have radios, newspapers, TV or any real contact with anyone other than themselves. There aren't any phones here, no way to communicate to the outside. Davis, so excited, explained the beauty of it. The solitude and completeness of being in a Christian community. Like the Book of Acts he said, whatever that means. Complete isolation so that the word of God can wash over them, cleanse them, make them new. What the fuck is wrong with the original? And how do they know what the new is. Who the fuck tells them what the new is? Can't be a spontaneous individual enlightenment as that would be too random. This is anything but random this is robotic. There's a book that tells them exactly what the new is. And a person, Liam, who interprets the book. Scary as shit. Makes me feel better about my last couple of years - my journey down the dark road to nowhere. At least it's honest.

I reach the trail that leads to Zion. The boundary is visible ahead, the wire fencing stretches up the hillside and down toward the pasture. Lily is stopped near the boundary line. I catch up but stay well behind her, wait. I want to tell her to fuck it, to just walk off and never look back but I don't. Finally I realize she's not going anywhere, she's not crossing over to the other side.

"What're we waiting for?" I call out. Lily is silent for a long time.

"For the Lord to tell me what to do. I'm not moving until I hear the voice of the Lord."

"The horses might get hungry before that happens," I joke, but she's not having it.

"You might get hungry before that happens too. You should go on, you can put Vienna up, the brushes are just inside the tack room door to the right and you'll see where the saddles and bridles go. There's hay down in that open area, she goes in the large pen. In fact you can take Maggie too." At that she dismounts, takes the reins over Maggie's head.

"I think I'll just wait with you, if it's all the same," I say. She gets back up on Maggie and just sits there. "Do you have your eyes closed?" I ask. "Can I catch up or will that disturb your prayer?"

Now I'm curious.

"You can catch up. And no, my eyes aren't closed. I'm waiting on the Lord, that's all."

"I honestly have no idea what that means." I catch up and stand beside her on Vienna. Vienna is taller than Maggie so I'm looking down at her as she is looking down. I can't see her face but her hands are busy, tapping out a rhythm, too busy. I imagine her mind is just as busy. "You stopped right before the boundary where the land changes. Did you realize that?"

"Yeah, I know. I like it up here, now I know. It's peaceful, or more peaceful."

We sit in silence a long time. I like being on Vienna, it's been a long time since I was on a horse and I miss it. I forgot how much I like riding horses, being around horses, smelling horses.

"I grew up with horses on the reservation. We always had horses to ride and we learned to take them out on the plains on our own as young kids, even before we started school. But we didn't have barns like here, the horses were free roaming and for some reason always just stayed close. I remember galloping across what felt like an endless expanse of golden land. It wasn't that endless by then, after the Wasichus cut it up, but it felt like it when I was little.

"We pretended we were on a hunting party, following the herd, riding with the Tatanka Oyate, the Buffalo Nation, riding inside the herd. Then making prayers for the one who offered its life so the people could live; offering tobacco, singing the Tatanka Olowan, the Buffalo Song, making prayers with the Buffalo Song. You have to be brave to hunt them, they're powerful and run like the wind. The horses have to be brave too. Shunka Wakán, sacred dog. That's what we thought horses were when we first encountered them. Shunka Wakán Oyate, the Horse Nation. I miss them.

"And you said your prayers while singing?"

"No, well yes, the songs are the prayers. The songs are hundreds of years old, some thousands. They're given in dreams or visions - during ceremony. The buffalo song, was lost for several generations, then a young warrior on his Hanblecia - his vision quest - was given that song again. When he came down from the mountain after his ceremony he shared it in the Inipi and one of our elders heard it. He said he remembered it from his own childhood but it had been lost for generations. That's how it was given back to us, songs are sacred, songs are prayers."

"I like that, that the songs are prayers. Sometimes it doesn't make sense to always be asking for something, or thanking and praising. Sometimes it just makes sense to sing."

On her horse Lily is slight but strong, she'd have been a warrior woman in my tribe. Her hair shines red in the sunlight, soft curls spill out of a bandana onto her shoulders. In another life I would have wanted to get closer.

"I . . . I can't make myself go down. Back there on the road, when we met up with the . . . the . . . with them, I saw them differently. They weren't brothers of one mind, as we say, instead they just seemed gullible or . . . . It's like the shining glow that shimmered around everything and everyone suddenly vaporized and what I saw was flat. Flat and kind of awful. I don't know what to do so I want to wait, in case God speaks. Until God speaks. And what if . . . . He doesn't? doesn't come, doesn't speak? I don't know what I'll do. It's this spot right here, where we crossed onto the BLM land. That's when everything started to shift. Maybe if I cross back everything will shift back to the way it was. I'll shift back to before . . . . Maybe I'll get my faith back."

"You sure you want it back? You don't sound convinced." Lily doesn't answer and she doesn't move. We sit like that for a very long time until the horses get restless.

Wade

❖

I ride back in the bed of the truck all wedged up against the sides with the brothers and the quartered elk and the head, antlers and hide between us in the middle. Grocery stores and refrigerated packaged meat, this I understand. This elk in parts, bloody and skinned on the bed of the truck, the exhilaration of the hunt and this sudden unexpected gift from God, this I've never known. Sawyer laughing now and at ease, jostling Marty, entertaining us all with tales of their pursuit. We made it down the trail with all of it.

"Have to hang it two weeks before we can eat it otherwise it's too gamey. Out back'a the toolshed with cheesecloth. Have to get a few hanging sacks for that."

Sawyer and Marty are all business now we're back at Zion. Working together with glances and nods, they get the quarters down off the truck quickly while the other brothers look to Paul, mill about, waiting to see what he will do. Paul nods to Andrew to help them pull a front quarter out of the truck bed and the rest begin helping as well.

"Before we hang it we'll want to take the back strap," Sawyer says. "That's the choice piece and we should have it tonight with the brethren. It'll be gamey but it's the best cut and is usually eaten the day of the hunt. We should celebrate."

Malcolm the tool steward, joins us out beside the truck, brings out a pile of crusty, bloodcaked cheesecloth sacks and begins pulling them apart. Sawyer and Marty work with the body parts, covering them up inside the cloth sacks. "I've used these a couple of times," Malcolm says. "No holes in them yet. Not much chance the flies will be a problem this time of year but you can't be too careful."

Julian

❖

Down below, coming from Zion, the sounds of the men in the truck drift up to us. There is laughter and a bunch of Praise the Lords. I can hear Davis' voice among them congratulating and giving his own Amens. Lily slumps in the saddle, rubs Maggie's neck, comforts the mare and then leans forward wrapping her arms around Maggie's neck and holds there. Maggie raises up her head and unsettles Lily. Then Lily closes her eyes, lightly squeezes Maggie's sides, and walks. Slowly, with eyes closed, she crosses the border into Zion and stops.

"Here, it was just here wasn't it?" She says without turning, eyes closed.

"Yes."

She turns, opens her eyes, stares at me for a long time, says nothing. I can tell by her expression that the faith didn't come back. Without speaking she looks away and continues down the trail. At the barn we untack the horses, groom then feed them, clean the tack. Lily works in silence on her regular chores; adding more shavings to the stalls, breaking the ice that has accumulated on the water trough. I ask if there is anything I can do and without looking up, in a voice that I hardly recognize she says that I can bring down a bale of hay from the loft, just toss it out the doors over the edge. Her voice is flat, monotone, disconnected.

Davis comes out to the barn eventually, asks if I want to stay for dinner and Bible study. I have no idea what happened. Lily won't talk anymore, it's like she's gone somewhere else and disappeared.

>   *"This is war. This is what we do. This is war, this is what we do. This is what we do, this is WHAT WE DO. this is war. this is what we do."*
>
>   *It's what he said when he saw I'd killed my first man. The eyes of a man who had killed more menwomenchildren than he could count were assessing me with their empty stare. The eyes of a man who believes this is what we do. Why? Because this is war.*
>
>   *"Do you hear me soldier?"*
>   *"Yes, sir."*
>   *"That's not good enough. I want you to say it and say it and say it. Over and over until you believe it. Because it's the only truth you need to know. Do you hear me now soldier?"*
>   *"Sir, yes sir. Sir, yes sir. Sir, yes sir."*
>   *Until finally I did believe it*
>   *until finally she did believe it.*

Sawyer

❖

Heat inside the tool shed burns like fire after the freeze. Hands and toes burn like coals. In the dim light of the tool shed Marty and I wait out the burn, not ready yet to return fully to life in the ministry, life with the brethren, the busyness and hustle of always doing.

"I'll never forget what we did yesterday and how we survived last night," Marty says. "Life in the suburbs didn't prepare me for that - the rush of it all. Still can't feel my toes though."

"You just wait until dinner tonight the back-strap and the other piece we saved out will feed us tonight. Everyone will benefit from this hunt. It feels good serving the Lord this way. Moving out of the usual. Stepping out to the immediate, the call of the Lord."

"Malcolm, you ever take down an elk? This ain't my first but it felt like it. With a knife. Never hunted elk with just a knife. The brethren're gonna feast. Can't wait until the rest of this meat's ready to roast. You up for a pit-fire?"

"Yeah, sounds good to me but Liam's not happy with you two taking off like that . . . just saying. Like you guys just off and left the work party. Moving that pig barn was no easy task. I watched it all from here."

"Off and left? You mean like listening to the Lord?"

"More like you disobeyed the Lord by walking off on the work party. And taking Marty with you. Leading one of God's lambs astray. Not me, I don't believe that, just heard it said."

"Hmm. Do you feel led astray Marty?"

"Of course not. Moment by moment we were led by God."

"Fu . . . hmm. You'd think some people'd be grateful but some people aren't able to acknowledge other people's talents."

"Well, just be warned."

"See if he'd come and say it himself. That's what I want to see. But ya know what? Fuck this all. I don't need this."

"You might want to watch yourself, uh, your tongue."

"Yeah? Well fuck you too. This ain't the real salvation. I know what the real salvation looks like an' this ain't it. You take care of yourself Marty. But I'm outa here."

So that's it then. Bring in food to feed the people for a season and this is it. Kicked out onto the street in the cold and rain. In the fucking freezing coldest nights of the year. Where's the 'love' we all talk about, preach about?

The wood chip trail back to the dorm winds through the stand of firs behind the tool shed. My stuff fits inside my sleeping bag and I'm gone. Hitch a ride to Illyria and I'm done.

"Sawyer!" Paul calls out just as I step out the dorm door. "Where you off to?"

"Where do you think."

"I need to talk to you first. Wait up, don't make me chase you."

"Do what you want but I'm not about to be rebuked by the likes of you."

"I come as a servant of the Lord. Anointed by God and you are in sin. Your acts against the Holy Spirit and Jesus cry out against you. You can still repent. Stand before the brethren and repent. I know you believe you are in the right but that's the point, none of us are in the right we are all in sin and in need of forgiveness."

"And Liam couldn't come himself? That chickenshit."

"I can't pretend I didn't hear that."

"Not asking you to. Brother."

"So what will it be? Are you ready to stand before the brethren, confess your sins. Repent of your ways, your willful disobedience to God's anointed?"

"As in you? God's anointed? You put yourself above the rest of us as though you have a direct line of communication."

"Not at all but I've been put in this position and I pray daily, hourly, to the Lord to fulfill his word. And yes, Liam did ask me to talk to you. This can't stand, this disobedience. And your attitude is the worst part of it. The action of disobedience is only a symptom of your attitude. You are convicted of sin."

"So . . . ah . . . no. No, no, no, I'm not going before everybody and debase myself for your need to have a full and complete order of obedience here with our little band of Christians. Who were they Annias? Sephria? Book of Acts, cast out for their sin. I know the drill. I'm leaving. But in full view, not in the night.

Lily

❖

The dining hall vibrates with the music of gratitude and praise, Bernie's fire backlights Liam as he speaks, his head haloed by the glow through his white hair. The guitar and the hum of soft notes are background to his words. Never a moment of silence never a moment of stillness. Charlie, off to the side and all the way at the back of the room, lets out a snore before Andrew elbows him awake. Liam shoots him a deadly glare before continuing.

"Can two walk together unless they be agreed? Are we one in Christ? Are we able to serve the Lord with false prophets among us? No. Know that Sawyer is marked and we will have no more fellowship with him."

"Amen."

"Praise the Lord."

But nothing about Marty. He sits quietly off to the side in the farthest back corner, head down, gripping the edge of the table, white knuckles, frozen. His innocence is not questioned, the new born in Christ, the lamb who was deceived by the whisperings of Sawyer, the tool of the devil. He's treated like a wounded lamb, honored for his service to the Lord and elevated for his commitment to the Gospel.

On and on the voice and the music, on and on filled to the brim with words from the book words defining reality. I am this narrative, this reality, inside the book. It is me, I am it. But I stood outside for just that one moment. Looked back over the threshold and now wonder how am I still here? For in truth, my brain is exhausted with manipulating the reality in front of me to fit with the Biblical. Working it all out, making it fit, fixing it so it all comes together, a perfect fit and an irresistible narrative, putting it all to words, children's stories easy to hear, simple to understand. Our job is to be a vessel, yielding always yielding at any moment our sinful nature brought to heel by . . . to the whims of . . . .

And but for Julian I did it, Julian the actual flesh and blood person who simply rode the back of a horse and sang his prayers. Who is closer to what feels like God than I've ever come by memorizing texts and opening myself up to my newness, my born again newness.

Weariness creeps up from behind, threatening to wash over the whole effort with sleep. Waiting for the voice of, the voice of . . . Christ? But the background music and the drone of Liam's voice are tootoo intrusive if only he would stop talking, if only they would stop singing and strumming. Then I could hear the voice of God, the voice of my . . . soul?

But this empty room rises up, a white room, a vision I see these days when I pray. And tonight the brethren and the guitar and Liam droning on and on. Inside the white room - empty, barren of furniture, the white walls stark and barren of art, windows, a door - Christ standing in the distant corner facing away. He refuses to acknowledge me, refuses to speak. And inside my chest this black sludge. A tarry well of blackness. The opposite of God's light? And yet I hold to this blackness. Deep in my bones I know if I let it go I lose my self, lose my soul.

If it just didn't come from so many directions at once then I would be able to find my footing. But the point is to not find my footing, that's the point of all this moving around. From California to Georgia, to Alabama, to Washington then back to California and then way out to Ohio and Illinois and Wisconson and now back out here to Zion so I would only have my footing in the Lord, in the book, in the ministry. No deep friendships no familiar place. In the world but not of it. But my feet crave dirt. Just that. Only that. Dirt and quiet.

Julian rode beside me on Vienna, in his ease on Vienna, in his ease with himself, with the earth, with dirt and with something more than words in a book. More than the teachings of words in a book. More than a way of life developed in response to teachings of words in a book. More than belief in a man who more than anyone ever, Ever, understands the exact meaning of words in a book. Without the layers of explanation and condemnation and exhortation . . . .

Whiteness searing into stillness. Holding onto breath, to the rise and fall of my chest, holding my focus on the wood grain of the table before me, the place where two veins meet, where tiny, long forgotten initials etched into the table before me are the only thing keeping me from flying out in all directions. Disappear into stillness, into nothingness. Hold on against the knowing that won't be denied that sets itself against, against ... But this raging torrent cannot be denied, cannot be controlled nor the urge to just start walking. Just walk. Not by all the efforts to stillness. Not by all the effort. It shifts and turns against me it roars like fire, a raging fire a raging ocean a raging . . . then laughter. That same laughter because I know I am the fool.

Julian simply rode beside me on Vienna and in relation with something I work so hard to accomplish . . . .

This should not happen out here in the sanctity of Zion. The safety of Zion. This is our place apart and where I thought I wouldn't have to think about things. Like the breathing earth or the urges of dreamstates, or the right and wrong of what? My faith? My surrender to Him?

The breathing earth. What was that?

The breathing earth. I felt it. I remember the breath of it still.

                                   The land changed

          right there just there where Zion ends
                 and BLM begins.
                          The one, then the other.
  Liam's voice and the singing duo, back and forth overlapping the walls golden

                                      the flames bright
      Liam striding backandforth a shadow now and
 and
 words
songs
words
too many words

"Where's the voice of God in all this sound? God is drowned."

A voice, my voice? shouting?

"Must find space must find air, too hard to breathe - out out."

"Lily." Liam's voice, a whisper. "Stay with me, Lily. Open your eyes and stay with me." Then hands touch head shoulders back and all around I feel the breath of those praying, mumbling words, prayers in other tongues. "Get thee behind me Satan, in God's name I cast thee out."

PART II

Lily

❖

The excuse I tell myself - head out to the trail to train Maggie, train her to be a reliable mount on any terrain, under any circumstance so she's safe for any rider - is what say to myself each day as I head out through the trees and up the deer trails that have now become horse trails. I believe this and yet somehow I always end up at the BLM boundary. And each time I cross the boundary line and step onto BLM land I quietly celebrate that I can breathe more freely, that I re-experience an opening of the chest - the feeling of connection to the land, to the earth.

And too I am still drawn to Marty and Sawyer's camp. This camp is less foul but the stench of death still lingers down as far as the dirt road. Vultures circle overhead, three today, less than I've seen before. Maggie makes herself big and readies for a bolt from the smell as we reach the trailhead: The spot where the brothers left the dirt road and hiked up, where they found Sawyer and Marty.

A light rain seeps through gloves and jacket and I want to

turn back but I just got here and I need to work with Maggie. We walk back and forth past the trail head, I on the ground leading Maggie. I, her lead mare, the one who protects her, who provides nourishment for her and who she trusts to keep her safe. I lead and she follows. With the halter and rope I brought along I tie her to a sturdy tree and walk up the trail.

The tracks from the brothers have faded with time, but the fire pit is still visible and the ground still littered with dried entrails, bones and fir. The smell of death this close brings up a dread I've not experienced before - the reality of death, the physical part not the Biblical 'overcoming of death' part. I understand Maggie's reaction, a primal awareness of danger, an ancient instinct, the bedrock of being, the real of what is. In the immediacy of death and dismemberment I feel an odd sense of wholeness. We are taught that the law of sin and death is overcome by the law of the Spirit because of Jesus, because of His sacrifice on the cross, the good news, that's the teaching. That's the first teaching, the first and most important teaching and meaning of salvation. But face to face with the stench of death in my nose my clothes my skin - nothing is more primal, more real. Deep in the marrow real and a truth not taught, retaught and not required to learn, not a concept to unravel for the deeper meaning. Just this instinctual response. Just this. Truth. No teaching. No stories. No words. Primal, instinctual, human.

Something missing these past four years cascades down around and through - a memory of lost inner cohesion, of integrity. Some part of me wants to turn back and un-know this moment, this camp. But the greater part brings me back here over and over.

The day I accepted Jesus and the stories of the Bible, the logic of it snapped into place with the God and the Devil in their roles of savior and deceiver made clear. With my entire past obliterated because it was all of the devil. With the stories of Noah and Moses and all, stories that up to that moment had no more hold on me than Santa or the Easter Bunny, now expected to serve as the foundation of my reality. But I heard it and I couldn't un hear it. I hated the very idea of it and fought it. I cursed it because I heard the logic of it and couldn't un hear it and I couldn't live with myself as a hypocrite so I gave in to it.

Too much LSD and too many nights on the road set me up. Set me up. But I didn't feel it. I didn't know what to say when the sister asked, "isn't it wonderful to be free from the power of sin and death? Isn't it amazing to feel the love of Jesus in your heart?" I didn't understand at all. I didn't feel any of it. So I got real serious about reading and studying what the Bible said. I just knew if I read enough it would all make sense. Reading, studying, reading studying readingstudying until it did make sense but the disconnect never left me. The Bible didn't speak the language of my soul - it always required translation. "Cast out the devil, get thee behind me Satan," they prayed, and all I could think was, *I turn my back on this blackness at my peril.*

A coyote ambles into the camp, unafraid of my presence and scavenges one of the remaining bones. She lays down and gnaws, trying to open the hard calcified bone and get at the marrow. The memory of Julian riding Vienna washes over me as I watch this beautiful animal, so alive in her element. So natural, so at peace, so at one in this element of predator and prey. No guilt, no morality sermon, no expectation that she should suddenly do otherwise because her nature is sinful. Julian a coyote among us. Then, with the long bone in her jaws she trots off sideways, dragging it down a thin, barely visible trail.

Maggie keeps turning away from Zion as we make our way back. Horses can find their way back in the dark, in a snow storm and with a blind rider on their back but Maggie keeps turning the wrong way. Eventually I decide to let her take me to wherever she seems to be heading.

Andrew

❖

Chores go by swiftly in the warm Spring air. Brothers working outside the sisters' dorm doing finish work, adding caulking to the windows. Then inside the dorm, caulking in one of the two bathrooms. Small cubicles line both sides along the length of the dorm. In each cubicle are two bunk beds and four dresser drawers, enough for each to have one drawer. Enough space and bunks for eighty sisters.

"The work is progressing on schedule," Liam says during his walk through. "Oh, and congratulations Andrew, you and Lily make perfect sense. I wondered when she would settle down, get married. Good for you."

"Thanks."

Finally life in focus. Lily my fiancé, out there on the horses. Soon she will be inside, in my cabin, caring for me and then my children. A boy and a girl.

"God told me she was mine, that He had given her to me, a gift, for the dedication I showed Him. My blessing on earth. It's God's will."

"Can't argue with that," Liam says.

Eating alone, instant in prayer, the dining hall still warmed by a small fire. The weight of responsibility on my shoulders.

"Congrats," Wade says, from behind. "I didn't know you and Lily even knew each other. Never seen you guys together, but hey, good for you."

Soon a married man, a married couple in the Lord. Raising children to follow Christ and His teachings. The blessing of it, the challenge of it.

Lily and the sisters together, talking, not sure I like their fellowship, I'll have to nip it in the bud.

"Lily, where have you been all morning? I need to talk to you. Out by the creek?"

"I was out with Maggie. Why by the creek? Why not here?"

"It won't take long."

"But we need a chaperone," she says. Now she's the proper one - now. But not then, not before, not out in the woods on the horses . . . .

"Not today," I assure her.

"Okay, but just for a few minutes. I have work to do here and lunch break is almost over."

The woods now even more fragrant with daffodils and lilacs, blackberries in bloom and ripening and wild azaleas. The creek is running high where the trail meets it so I take us up-creek to a sandy area out from under the canopy of firs. The sand is warm from the morning sunshine. Even the day celebrates my marriage. We stop beside the creek, listen to the sound of the water. Christ turned water into wine and I will turn Lily into the most virtuous woman in the ministry. She will be the wife everyone praises and I will be the husband honored for her virtue.

"The Lord spoke to me, Lily. It's something I've been praying about for a long time and then the Lord spoke, He gave His promise to me. That we two will be married. It's His will that you will be my helpmeet and I your husband and that during our first year it will be my job to comfort you in all the days of your vanity."

Lily's silence is all I need to know that we two will be married. "It's a good day in the Lord when two can walk together. And with Christ as my head it is a threefold cord not easily broken."

"I have to get back," Lily says. "I have chores to do."

Lily walks on ahead. Watching her now, my helpmeet, I finally see her for the bride she will be. I'll find out if we have to do the usual six months separation and waiting period or if Liam will just let it slide. Probably will since we're here at Zion. And her with the horses and all. Of course that will change with her being married and all. A woman's place and all. Praise the Lord. Amen and amen.

> *As David took Bathsheba, it is for you to take Lily for your own. Claim her for your wife. Cleanse her of her sinful nature.*
> *As David took Bathsheba, it is for you to take Lily for your own. Claim her for your wife. Cleanse her of her sinful nature.*

> *As David took Bathsheba, it is for you to take Lily for your own.*
> *As David took Bathsheba, it is for you to take Lily.*
> *As David took Bathsheba.*

Liam

❖

Look around you, Andrew, here in Zion we are completely self sufficient. We see daily the hand of our Lord, and we are blessed because our walk is upright in the eyes of the Lord, as we yield our hearts and minds ... but what you say He has told you to do ... Andrew that is not of the Lord."

"But He showed, He spoke to me . . . I."

"Andrew, what you heard was not of the Lord. It's not possible that the Lord would tell you to take your sister in Christ like that."

"It's not consistent with our teachings, I know that but it is Biblical. And David did take Bathsheba and then he had her husband killed. Killed! and then married her and comforted her. And God's love for David never changed. Even then."

"But hasn't she agreed to the marriage? This doesn't make sense."

"He said I am to purify her, cleanse her of her sinfulness."

"Only Christ can cleanse us of our sins."

"My belly feels like it's being eaten by worms. This voice.

How long I've listened and trusted. How can I trust the Lord when His voice has turned against me, what He repeats over and over, I can't do it, I won't do it. It's of the Devil yet not."

"You know the Devil uses the Word of God to deceive."

"Then how do I know the difference?"

"What did Lily say? Didn't she agree to marry you? This doesn't make any sense."

"She didn't actually say one way or the other. I got ahead of myself before. I spoke out of faith but I hadn't asked her yet. Today though I did and I felt her soften."

"Then it's of the flesh. No doubt about it. Not the Devil. It's your own sinful nature stepping up. What you wanted but were able to hold back because of your dedication to the Lord. You're a strong brother, Andrew, and a leader. You'll be okay - pray, confess, fast if you're led. The Lord is a rock and you can trust Him."

"How can you know that? It feels the same as every other time God has spoken to me. His voice is strong and with it is a deep abiding peace I don't ever experience otherwise. It is my experience of Him in its fullness. This time is no different."

"Then where's the peace? Pray and fast, Andrew. The Lord will heal you and speak to you."

"Yes, okay, I'll do that."

"Go now, Andrew, go to the dorm, don't go back to work today. Give it time, give her time. See what she says in a few days. And in your case you two can marry as soon as you want. No waiting period."

"Yes . . . Okay."

Lily

❖

Some things just have to be worked out alone - outside the community of the brethren. Away from the constant voices of the brethren. The voice of Liam. The voice of Andrew. But there is no outside there is no away. Only this question of marriage and the vista from here that it might all change somehow, somehow be different. Somehow.

Andrew insisting it's God's will, Liam agreeing it's God's will and a reasonable marriage. So against all my instincts I agreed. And in three days I will be married.

Then in confidence Liam said, "I don't know what happens to these sisters when they get married. They suddenly turn into witches. I don't get it. Of course not you, Lily, I know that's not going to be the case with you." So I knew, then, I must be the exception and my walk must be blameless.

I expected the presence of the Lord to increase after my decision to live inside His will, to take this step to yield as a vessel to His will, like jumping off a cliff to find myself in His loving arms - my always protector and comforter. But His presence didn't increase, it became more and more distant and I am still falling, unable to catch any footing. There is no Comforter, no presence, and Jesus still is standing with his back to me, silent, obstinate. Obedience to the Lord, that's all that remains. Just that.

Since that day riding beside Julian the tender presence of Jesus is vanished. Riding out onto BLM land, listening to his easy words, watching the eagle come and greet him so casually as though it was the most natural thing in the world. And knowing that to him it was the most natural thing in the world. It's since then this all started. Like a veil lifted and the hazy sheen of loving the Lord shifted into this blank nothing. Leaving me with clarity and emptiness. "What does your soul want?" he asked when I told him I couldn't write poetry since becoming a Christian. Like a shaft of light focusing my vision, the reality of my own emptiness was clear in that moment. But I wanted to think his words away, think they meant nothing I fought to believe they were nothing, just nothing. But I knew it wasn't true.

So tonight I walk the earth to listen, and to feel this lake of tar that still lives inside me. A last act outside the bond of marriage, the bond of obedience. If I don't listen to this darkness all that will remain will be the blank white wall. And salvation through obedience. Salvation through obedience. Not enough, it is not enough.

I wish Cass was here. Living all this time this in the ministry, Liam's wife, but somehow able to maintain herself. Her and Julian, Indian way he said. She would know with her snark and her anger, her edge against her rejection of the Lord. Just five minutes to find out how she does it in the midst of this overwhelming; that God is with us that this is the true the only that we are the chosen that, that . . . I wish she was here. She would know about this black sticky stuff.

In three days a wedding.

Walking the trail, touching the earth with bare feet, not on Maggie, Tony, or Vienna. Just feet, bare feet. Why does it feel forbidden? Why does it feel so good? Moonlight on my shoulders, soft, dark earth between my toes. The simple act of touching the earth of wanting to feel the earth breathe once again. Deeper into the woods and the sweet smells of the forest rise up, smell of honey, smell of pine. The sound of the creek burbles with the spring thaw, warm and fragrant. Perhaps the condemnation comes from just this, this act of touching, of feeling . . . no, of *knowing* the earth. This is forbidden because we say we are separate from the earth, we are called upon to step outside and name and categorize her and objectify her - to plow, domesticate, dominate her. Yet in the shelter of the woods and on BLM land my chest relaxes, I breathe more freely. And remember her name, Julian told me her name is Uncí Makáh.

In three days.

Cass

❖

Sawyer reminds me that there really is no difference between myself and Liam. We both believe we know better than anyone the right way everyone else should live. He straddles the fence though, between Zion and his own childhood religion; play acting at being free from Zion but unable to accomplish what feels like a walk with Christ. So he lives in guilt. Second guesses himself all day and night until he's tied in knots. Easier if he just returned to Zion. These white men and their white ideas rub against something inside that always feels raw and open. A wound that can't heal. Tell me who I am Liam, tell me what to do Liam, tell me the meaning of my life, Liam, tell me, tell me, tell me.

"When're you com'n back out to Illyria?" Sawyer asks when I gather the groceries - my excuse to spend time away from Zion.

"I don't know, maybe tomorrow, maybe next week. Maybe next month."

"You know Julian right?" Sawyer asks. "He's coming by. I met up with him not long after I left Zion. He remembered me from when I brought down the elk. I remembered him too but couldn't remember where from. We've become good friends, now there's someone who isn't haunted."

"Why would you say that?"

"He's like a cat. Relaxed in his skin. Eats when he wants, sleeps when he wants, does absolutely nothing for long stretches and feels no guilt. Then without any apparent effort gets moving and accomplishes something real. Quite the example after being driven like a mule these past years. I can only wonder what that feels like."

"So you admit you're not clear of the whole sin and death thing. I guess I thought you thought . . . oh well, never mind."

"No, I know I'm backslidden and it's hell, can't find it in me to fully believe in God after the ministry. Still, though, shame and confusion covers everything. Need an AA meeting or something just to walk down the street. Or RA - Religion Anonymous - ha. Like tentacles wrapped around my chest. I can't outrun the guilt. Beginning to think the truth of it is what we were doing. The whole truth of it, Zion, the houses, our belief that we finally hit on the real interpretation that others missed, beginning to think we actually knew. That we were right."

"Or maybe the truth of it is that it was a mind fuck from the beginning and you still need to find your way out."

"Julian's here. Your relative if I'm not wrong. Hey, Julian look who's here."

Julian comes in, shakes my hand, then Sawyer's. Traditional, feels good to be around Julian, around n'dn ways. Offers Sawyer some tobacco after. Feels very good.

"Sawyer told me you were coming out today," Julian says. "How's Lily these days? Last I saw her she kind of shut down. But before that we had some good talks. Good horses out there. Too bad it's all out there. Maybe we could cook her up in a lodge. That would heal what needs healing. If she'd do it."

"She's getting married very soon unless she backs out. A sorry thing if you ask me."

'What? Who to?"

"Andrew."

"No way. That can't be, that's the exact opposite of what she should do. Maybe I can come back with you, try to reason with her. Either way she should sweat."

"That's not going to happen. Liam would never let her off Zion," Sawyer says. "How on earth did that happen? They didn't even talk, I didn't think they even knew each other."

"It was 'God's will' according to Andrew and Liam. And she went along with it. She seems flatlined though. Andrew doesn't notice of course but the light has gone out of her. She spends most of the time up in the woods, so some part of her is still alive."

"She's finding her healing out there then. We can sweat her out in the little lodge you set up off the land. No one will even know she's gone."

The long drive back to the Zion in the early days of Spring have always reminded me why I love this land. Lately though the mid-day sun on the lake shimmers nervously and the mountains stand guard against something unknown. Too different from the sacred Black Hills, those soft, gentle guardians.

Julian

❖

Standing on the dirt road at the edge of the pasture by the horse barn the place is changed. Everything looks different in the spring. Purple irises blanket the area between the barn and the pasture and around the edges of the woods. Sunlight shines deep into the woods along the trail in dapples, inviting entrance. Lily canters Vienna around the edge of the pasture while a young foal races ahead, kicking and bucking.

One glance in my direction and nothing so I walk out onto the sloggy grass and wave. Nothing. But her body tenses up and Vienna breaks into a rough trot. This is what broken looks like. This is the flatline Cass mentioned and what I saw that day as we came down out of the hills after finding Sawer. But animals know and Vienna betrays her.

"I know you see me," I call out when she brings Vienna down to a walk, making a great effort to avoid looking in my direction.

"What are you doing out here?" She says, finally walking up beside me.

"Heard you were getting married to Andrew."

"This week."

"You don't exactly look thrilled. Are you sure it's what your soul wants?"

Her face twists up then returns to the mask so quickly I would have missed it if I wasn't staring so hard. Vienna swishes her tail in response to the tension, side steps and bundles up her haunches to spin and bolt. Lily is quick enough to fake relaxation and stop her but the reality is clear enough to both of us.

"What do you know about what my soul wants?"

"Listen to your horse if you won't listen to your heart."

"Who brought you out here this time? Not Davis. I know that because he hasn't been around for a few months. Was moved to the Chicago house, I think."

"Cass, she told me you were getting married to Andrew and we, she and I, thought it would be good if I came out, see if you wanted to sweat first."

"How'd you meet up with Cass?"

"Long story, but what about a sweat?"

"I don't know what that means."

"It's a ceremony. One of the Lakota ceremonies. Cass has a lodge by the creek out on the far side past the garden. She's preparing it for you. Now. Smell the smoke?"

I point with my lips toward the spot in the woods Cass showed me. "The smoke is visible now, it's just the initial flare up from lighting the fire. Once it gets going the smoke disappears and only the sweet fragrance of the smoke remains. That's the beauty of the Inipi fire, that it hides itself from prying eyes."

Lily

❖

Julian steps out from behind the barn like a ghost. Seeing him again after all this time my stomach churns and I wonder at his beauty, at how much I've thought about him and that I feel this way just days before I'm to marry Andrew.

I wonder if he remembers me.

Vienna breaks into a trot and I bring her down to a walk.

"I know you see me," he calls out. "I know you know me."

Impossible longing grips my heart but I resist, call it sin, think hard on sin and death and Hell and, and . . . But this longing is so deep and resonant it must be sin and it is sin, I tell myself. Julian is of the Devil and that's why I feel so deeply. But I don't believe a word of it.

"Cass has set up a ceremony for you on the other side of the creek, off Zion but close by. She wants you to come before your marriage. It's just outside the boundary of Zion. Where the earth breathes. Where you felt it."

Where I felt, where my heart opened. My secret place I go

to, to feel. Where the black sludge calls the loudest.

And this stepping into the unknown, knowingly stepping off the forged path and onto this dirt path - allowing myself to get lost that I might find my self back, is this so evil? Must I always live with this stabbing condemnation that tightens and crushes so that I can hardly breathe? Am I required to obliterate myself, give myself away? This solid wall of rejection of all things outside our ministry is beginning to show cracks. So I agree to this time with Julian and Cass, and accept that I actually do want something.

"Good, Cass has it all set up for you. I'll put Vienna up while you get ready. Bring a skirt to wear in the lodge and change of clothes for after, and, oh, are you on your Moon?"

"What? Oh, I get you, no."

"And bring a towel. I'll wait by the bridge and we'll walk over. I'll show you where."

We cross the bridge, hug the creek on the far side and keep going until we just cross the BLM boundary line and there it is, a fire and a small igloo like structure covered with blankets. Cass sets a few pieces of wood on the fire, stacks it up like a little teepee. Between the pieces of wood are red glowing rocks and coals.

"Glad you came," she says, reaching forward to shake my hand - which she's never done before. Hesitantly I shake her hand. A soft touch. Something my dad once described as holding a wet fish. "This," she nods toward our handshake, "is traditional way of greeting. It's part of our ceremony. We do it to make relations, touch to touch. A way of showing respect and of finding that connection, flesh to flesh. Not like white people way of showing dominance with a firm, bone crushing grip."

Cass is wearing a long skirt, something else I've not seen before. Most all the sisters wear long skirts almost all the time but never ever Cass, except for now. On her head is a bandana and around her neck she wears a small leather pouch that I've also never seen before. Suddenly it's so obvious that she's Indian.

"Come, stand by the fire," she says. "It will help you get used to the heat so when you go inside the lodge it won't surprise you.

And make relations with the Inyan, the Stone People, while we wait for them to get ready. Take this tobacco, offer it to the Inyan, introduce yourself, tell them why you've come."

The stones are glowing red and the heat is intense. Julian stands right up to the edge of the fire with his tobacco, spends a long time there speaking quietly, looking at the stones, making prayer? I move up close after he leaves, follow his example, introduce myself. I think about what to say to tell them why I've come and suddenly all the feelings I've been so successful at pushing away are upon me. Tears come and I want to step back and get away except that now, as I look at the stones, they're old, ancient, timeless. And they have a name, Inyan. It feels like speaking to a friend - one who can listen and hear what I'm afraid to say. I want to stay close to them but the heat burns my face fiercely so I sprinkle my tobacco and step back.

"Why tobacco?" I ask Cass when she comes over to make her own prayers.

"That's a story for inside the lodge," she says. "Did you bring a change of clothes? A towel? You'll get cold after if you don't have something dry to change into. Bring the towel into the lodge, you'll find out why once we get started."

When the fire shifts and the stones drop Julian says they're ready and steps behind some trees, changes into swim trunks and then crawls into the lodge through the small opening.

"Kneel down and crawl in going clockwise until you're at the very back opposite the door - the honor seat," Cass says, smiling. "Before you go in say, Mitakuyas or 'all my relations,' it's a way of acknowledging all those who are our relatives - the green and growing, the four legged, the swimmers, creepy crawlies, the spirit nations, the Inyan who you've already met, and your ancestors who have gone on to the spirit world. Just say it," she says when I step back.

Crawling in I speak the words and feel a strange connection, the Inyan and now the green and growing. The small, dark space is big enough for the three of us; the inside is made of curved branches and on the branches are tiny colored bundles of cloth hanging on red yarn.

Julian motions to Cass who then slides a stone through the door on a pitchfork. Julian guides it to a small pit in the center, nudges it off with deer antlers and settles it into place. The red hot stone radiates tremendous heat and this is only the first one. He sprinkles cedar on the stone, the Inyan, and says, "welcome Grandfather, thank you for coming. Pilamiyayelo, Tunkasila."

The fragrance is calming. I am ready.

Julian has not spoken except to instruct Cass to bring in the stones. Seven come in then Cass holds a bucket of water near the doorway. Julian motions for me to help and together we take the handle and bring the water over the stones before setting it down near the doorway. Cass crawls in and shuts the door flap.

Darkness like nothing I've experienced before, then a slow rhythmic drumbeat, a heart beat, then Cass singing and the sound of water moving then sizzling on the stones and then heat and heat and heat. I can't take my eyes off the glowing red stones. As the color fades and the heat rises I move to get away but the movement sears my skin so I hold still, breathe through my nose but the steam burns my nose then through my mouth but my throat is burning. All the while Cass and Julian are singing.

Wordlessness, pounding heartbeat, songs in a language I don't understand. A darkness so black it is bright so hot it is cold, so familiar it hurts. I want to stay and never leave. Here with Cass and Julian I feel at home and at ease for the first time in years, even in the searing. Slowly, carefully I raise the towel to my mouth, cover my nose and breathe, then sing along as best as I can.

The beauty of this place overcomes until I am weeping uncontrollably.

The flap at the doorway opens and Cass goes back out and brings in seven more red stones, all in silence. Be *attentive*, I hear. This voice speaks quietly like a dreamvoice, a whisper, I hear it and watch. Every movement, every nod has meaning, the very circle of this lodge has meaning. Above is another circle made with the branches, a circle just above the circle where stones rest. It is the womb of the earth and I am within her. Julian closes the doorflap again and with the drum begins another song.

I can't help but pray in tongues, my spirit language. My heart language. And in this language it is my heart that leads, not my mind. No thought just heart and I move along a path of loved ones; my little brother who I haven't seen in four years; my parents who love me in spite of my evangelizing; my old friend Gabe who I walked away from after the year and a half on the road where he had carried me, protected me in my innocence and ignorance of all things outside my sheltered family life; and now this man Julian who offers his tradition and his sacred ceremony so I can feel, and Cass who somehow walks in two worlds.

She opens the door two more times, adds seven more stones two more times. Four doors, no talking only the drum and the songs and the flow of prayers in my spirit language. The language of my soul? No talking at all.

"You did good, you're strong, a lot stronger than I expected," Julian says after.

"No words," I say. "How could you have known?"

"To speak is not forbidden but today what was needed was not my words or Cass's but the words of the sacred ones, the Inyan and Mni Wakán, the Sacred Waters. Together they speak and sing with the sacred breath. I like that you tried singing. You did good."

"I thought you would talk about . . . stuff."

"I came to pour water. The ceremony doesn't need us except to chop wood, carry stones and pour water, the ceremony speaks for itself."

Julian

❖

These fragrant hills with their endless green, again move in my limbs in my chest. Too many winters of deliberate oblivion and kinship ties deliberately deadened. Finally, again the horse nation, the elk nation, the fever of warmth after the Inipi. The fire in the chest and in the bones. Heat from Tunkasila and Makáh. Heat within and heat without. These years a waste but finally I know why here, why now. To feel the stone people again after I'd left them and looked for healing from another spirit. The spirit in the bottle that seduces with the ease of a mistress - one who asks nothing and gives all - until all is nothing but emptiness and shame and longing. Lily's prison was easy to see. Mine I didn't recognize until I saw hers and understood its power to obliviate, to steal the very life and soul. Now this, this call back to ceremony with the fierce hunger of the bear awakened after the long winter: Unexpected, unasked for. A trick of coyote nation who walks on my shadow, on my footprint and wanders off laughing. He always laughs. He reminds me of my cousins my aunties my dead brother. The one who fell before me and stayed down. The one who surprised us all with his determination to die. He ran to it like some kind of reward, some kind of race - who could get there first. Is that why I stayed in Illyria all this time? Waiting to join my brother? Waiting to plunge or rise or fly to the Milky Way? No, this is why - my return to ceremony and maybe for Lily. Lily in her effort to die; she seemed the fool but in the end she exposed my own death wish. Breathe in breathe out. Slow the heart beat. And now the circle is enlarged to contain me my ceremony my Inipi my fire my altar my Sundance my drum - all circles. Circles within circles within circles. Pilamiyayelo Wopila.

Ómakiyayo o-ay
Ómakiyayo o-ay
Ómakiyayo o-welo ay
Ómakiyayo o-ay

Tunkasala   Wakán Tanka
Ómakiyayo o-ay

Lily

❖

This evening, one of my last in the tent, the sisters want to celebrate with me but my heart is cold. I pretend though, laugh and talk, mostly nod. They hope they can find a husband as dedicated to the Lord as Andrew. They look forward to being a wife, a helpmeet for their husband, the fulfillment of a woman's life in the Lord and a time when her salvation can rest finally in the confidence that the man is the head and in her obedience to him she's no longer responsible for her salvation. These words of compliance send a cold shiver through me. It's something I had accepted but now after the Inipi with Julian and Cass it's the opposite of what I want.

When things wind down I dig deep into my sleeping bag - my private place, my refuge, my one constant these years in the ministry - try to feel its comfort and warmth. Instead I lie awake, wondering why I have agreed to this marriage, this throwing away of myself. Is it the effort to stop the doubt, the conflict, the wavering faith? Just step over the thresh hold, don't think - my salvation sealed, safe, secured by my marriage?

Andrew-the-head now responsible so I can't fall?

The picture I have in my head is of a warm and cozy place, dry and fragrant. The smell of bread baking and the sound of, the sound of. But there are no sounds in this place that I imagine. The loneliness frightens me. The picture in my head changes to an endless expanse of time in which silence reigns. Andrew and I don't talk to each other about anything important or about anything at all. The absolute loneliness of this warm cozy now terrifies and I want to smash it. Take a rock and smash it.

Silence. That state I've longed for these past months has apparently been given to me; a backhanded answer to my prayer. And didn't I know this all along? this anti-chemistry between myself and Andrew? Of course. How could I not recognize the awfulness of this. Because it was less awful than continuing the life of sisterhood. Time stretching forever onward in this unpredictable ministry of sisterhood.

"This way we live is not a democracy," Liam once said, "it's authoritarian rule in a communist state." We do what we're told as a matter of pride. We live in a cocoon - are nurtured, fed, given meaning and direction inside our cocoon. And in the case of women, we are at the beck and call of any brother who might want or need something. At any moment asked to change everything we've known or have become accustomed to and do something else, live somewhere else. Be someone else.

From deep inside my body a heat rises, the response to the lingering remanent of heat from the ceremony. My sleeping bag now a trap to escape. Escape the steaming, allow my body to take in the sweet chill of sweat drying; I can't get out of it quick enough. Sitting on the edge of the bunk, with eyes closed, I see the red stones again, hear the resonance of the drum, remember the clear surge of fear that followed the first time Julian added water to the stones. In my mind I saw the heat rise in the center of the Inipi, like red and singed air following a path. Fear then and then stillness, slow easy breaths and then stillness, peace, transcendence, stillness. Julian's voice, Cass's voice, my voice. Beauty-way, he said.

Refreshed and energized by the night air, I dress and barefoot walk out to the pasture. From here the night sky glitters brilliant. The Milky Way a stunning display in this dark land, the Bear quietly resting in the north. The horses are out of their stalls nibbling at hay that I put outside this evening. Maggie looks up and whinnies. This last piece of freedom, this air, this night wandering; this is it. The very last time I will know this freedom such as it is. I've come to appreciate the smallest things. The grand miracles in my life are really tiny wonders. This air, this night, the smell of the horses, the smell of the woods.

From the direction of the sister's tent I see a flashlight moving in my direction. One of the sisters coming to check on me? The light flashes in my eyes and it's impossible to see which sister it is. Blinded by the light even as she sits beside me I can't tell who it is. Then Andrew's voice whispering in my ear, very close. "You shouldn't be out here by yourself. It's not safe to be out in the dark." His hand on my throat, pressing down. Pushing down.

"Andrew stop it." I push his hand away but just as soon his hand returns with more pressure. I struggle to move away from him but can't find the traction while pinned at my neck.

"*As David took Bathsheba, it is for you to take Lily and claim her for your wife.* This is what the Lord said to me, Lily. He said that you are to be my wife and that I am to take you as David took Bathsheba. Do you understand? It is not for us to question the Lord."

"Take your hand off my neck."

"It is God's will."

"Take your hand off my neck now, Andrew. I will scream."

"No one can hear you. You made sure of that. You know it's okay, that's why you came out here. The sisters told me where to find you."

"No they didn't, I didn't tell anyone. Were you spying on me?"

"*As David took Bathsheba, it is for you to take Lily and claim her for your wife.*"

Andrew pushes me down and straddles me repeating the words over and over. I know rape and I know panic and I know what Andrew is doing and I won't give him the satisfaction of a conquered bride or whatever he thinks this is. "Andrew, let's not do this here," I whisper in his ear which is now right next to my face. "Let's go to the barn, the loft. It's soft and more private there. We can take our time there. Better to enjoy."

"You mean it?"

"Yes, let me up and let's walk over there. It's just a short walk."

"Good. Then you will be my betrothed and we will be married. As David took Bathsheba, it is for you to take Lily and claim her for your wife."

"But wait, I need to freshen up. You won't go anywhere will you? You'll wait for me won't you?"

"I'll wait right . . . Wait a minute, this is not God's will. You propositioning me here in the night. Whore!" he yells, then pushes me back down and tries to remove my jeans. "Whore!" He roars again, right into my ear. "You are the whore of Babylon. You will be cast into the lake of fire unless you have me to raise you up, a child unto the Lord. And now you must see that I am your only salvation."

But in his anger and his distraction he lifts himself just enough for me to slam the heel of my palm upward against his nose. Now howling and gasping he rises up and leans away, giving me just enough room to shove him completely away. Blood is streaming from his nose and he seems blinded by it.

"You drew blood," he yells at me as I run back toward the sister's tent. "I didn't draw blood but you did. You drew blood."

Inside the tent I move quietly so as not to disturb anyone, grab my shoes, my sleeping bag, my sweatshirt, my Bible and walk out the long driveway to the valley road. I will be blamed for this. Andrew's word against mine.

Wade

❖

"Andrew your nose is bleeding. What happened?"

"She's gone I know it. Something inside me knew it was coming all along. How did I know it was coming? the Lord has been so clear? But I knew. 'We are to be married,' He said. 'Because of your love toward Me and your absolute dedication to My Word I will reward you with Lily.' The perfect gift from my beloved Savior. But now this violence. But the Lord told me. I don't understand it."

"What are you talking about?"

"We were going to have our wedding on the pasture. Tomorrow morning, like the other brothers did. It's so perfect out there on the pasture. It's what we agreed to. It's what the Lord promised when He spoke to me. 'As David took Bathsheba, it is for you to take Lily and claim her for your wife.'"

"Wait, what? What did you say?"

"And that I was to raise her up in the Lord. Make her the perfect virtuous woman. Show all these rebellious sisters what a wife in the Lord can look like."

"No, no, no, not that, that part about about David and Bathsheba."

Anguished changes pass over Andrew's face in rapid succession, biting his lip, sucking up the blood from his mustache. He has not made eye contact since he sat down.

"Spit it out Andrew," I demand.

"It's what the Lord told me. And I finally had the faith to act on what God has been saying. I was strong in the Lord and of perfect faith, then she struck me. She drew blood. Probably broke my nose."

"Lily did this? Just now? What were you doing that she would do that?"

"The Lord told me. The Lord spoke to me. It was of the Lord."

"What was of the Lord? As David took Bathsheba? Did you rape Lily?"

"Of course not. God told me to take her. 'Take her' as David took Bathsheba. She became his wife and it was of God. Not rape. No, never. Plus she ran off. Right after she hit me. She might be gone."

"That's insane. You're out of your mind, Andrew."

Liam

❖

This is what this isolation leads to. I've told you before something like this was bound to happen when these young people have only this . . . this isolation. I don't know what else to say. All they know is what comes from you, your ideas, your expectations your interpretation. This is what it leads to Liam. Attempted rape! From these crazy notions that Andrew had in his head that it's God's will he should rape Lily? And you never saw it coming even when he said he should take her against her will because the voice in his head told him to? And that she would then become a child for him to raise? The man, the boy really, is sick and all you did was encourage him in his delusion."

Cass rages, as though it's my fault.

"Be silent woman! Andrew has fallen into false doctrine, a trick of the Devil, he's hurting but humble enough to be able to hear the voice of the Lord. I will take care of him, just as I take care of all the flock. I'll speak to him tonight. I'll send him to the St Louis house where he can heal under Jason's pastorship and away from Lily. Jason will help him through this. Andrew is a strong servant and one of God's future leaders. He can be healed of this. I'll talk to him."

"I can't believe it. Don't you see what you're doing here? You actively encourage this insanity. You, the infallible one, sit here, before all these young people, most barely out of high school, still children, and those still healing from war wounds, and you tell them stories that keep you in this lordly position of prophet and no one has the nerve to speak against you, not even the elders that you anointed. But I'm your wife and I will speak against you. I will expose you to the elders who hold their tongues. All the properties and the toys you have amassed at the expense of these young people while they live in tents. The good food we eat out here in secret while they eat mush and peanut butter. Nothing to say for yourself?"

"Get thee behind me Satan! I'll deal with you later. Right now you need to find Lily. Maybe she's out on one of the horses. Or out in the woods somewhere. It's not safe for her, she can't be alone."

"I'll look for Lily but not to tell her to stay near others and not be out alone, I'll tell her to leave. Leave this place."

"She can go to the house in Florence or anywhere else she choses while we sort this out."

"Hopefully she'll leave and just keep on going. You know she doesn't belong here. Never has. But you can't let go of any of them. Your sheep."

Andrew

❖

And in your nakedness and in your desolation I will make of you, Andrew, a new man. You will rise up from this place of confusion to become the most honored. And from this place of astonishment you will find order and a requiem of solace. Go forth and speak my words unto these people. These brothers and the sisters in your midst, who have rejected your words. My Words. Go in nakedness, true nakedness. As Jeremiah made my words into true acts of love toward me, so must you also take my words and speak out in your nakedness.

Speak unto me, oh Lord, and I will do thy will to speak against those who would reject the words you have given unto your servant. I am your servant and your word is upon my tongue. These clothes, a corruption from the world, I drop from my body to appear before the brethren in true nakedness.

And so in nakedness I now walk among the tents and the

cabins, among the brethren of Zion, calling out your words, the words you have spoken unto me;

> "Because you have not heard my words, because you have not yielded to the voice of my servant Andrew, behold I will send and take all the people of this Land.
>
> "I will stand against the inhabitants thereof, and will utterly destroy them, and make of them an astonishment, and an hissing, a perpetual sickness and a desolation.
>
> "Thus saith the Lord: If ye will not harken to me, to walk in my law, which I have set before you, o harken to the words of my servant Andrew the prophet whom I sent unto you; Then I will make of this house Shi-loh, will make this Land a curse to all the nations of the earth."

And so the people came. Just as you said oh Lord. They came to hear the voice of your prophet. And with robes and garlands they have covered your servant. And now I will be led to the place of honor as you so promised. "Amen, brothers?"

"Amen Andrew. Let's go to my trailer, I'll warm you up and you can talk more about what the Lord has been showing you." Liam, tonight like the father he has always been to me. The comforter in the absence of comfort. The voice of truth in the absence of truth in the sinful world.

Whispers among the brethren still in awe of the glory. One can not come away from an encounter with the Lord Himself unless one is changed as Moses was changed when he returned from the mount.

"Amen, brothers?"

"Amen, Andrew."

Lily

❖

Town is close, an easy hitch hike from Zion. I lived here before, it's where I became a Christian. It's where I watched the Christians handing out tracts. It's where I despised them and then joined them. It's where I landed after high school. That first summer after graduation, hitchhiking north like my life depended on it. To Big Sur then on to Mendocino, then, reaching Illyria, I stopped and stayed. Illyria - my rainsoaked escape from sunny California, from Hollywood and Disneyland. A place I thought might be more real than one created for tourists and voyeurs. Illyria in winter was a magnet. A place that drew certain people and kept them. Throngs of freaks and roadies thinking they were only passing through ended up staying.

Somehow when I drove in from Zion to buy equipment for the horses, no memories ever came. And when I came in with the brethren to evangelize, no memories came. But now when my ride lets me out near the University it floods back.

Some of the old magic returns. Unexpected excitement of moving into the unknown? And walking the streets feels good, walking, just that. Maybe this time hitch hike and walk, both. Trek south, eventually reach California and move sideways toward the mountains. Trek my way down to Mexico or back to Laguna visit my parents, start over somehow.

Passing frat house smells, their beer cans strewn on the sidewalk. How is this still happening? How has nothing changed? It seems a lifetime ago I lived here; passing these same noisy frat houses; watching this same drunken nighttime routine.

Up ahead the freaks at the far end of the avenue gather near a food truck and stand in line for fried rice; young women, hardly more than girls, in long skirts and Nehru style blouses or fringe jackets. Many are barefoot and a few wear work boots. Some dance nearby to the music that streams out of the truck speakers, the Grateful Dead and Santana, music I haven't heard since joining the commune. The dogs that stand near these young men and women are quiet and watchful, keeping their person safe and waiting for food. I forgot what it means to be on the street. To be on my own. Again that fleeting sense of magic and wonder. A reminder of the early days of adventure on the road.

Outside the New World I sit on the curb and watch cars and people pass by. How long has it been since I just sat and watched anything? The idleness of it scares me so I walk some more but I end up back at the New World. Must find safety must find shelter for the night must trust the Lord, that's all I know in spite of myself. Prayers and walking and again I am in front of the New World.

Then Julian's voice, but it can't be him. Not here. It speaks in a soft whisper. A face near my own just like Julian's.

"Lily, open your eyes, get up. Come inside and warm up."

I look up and there is no one there. No Julian. But I get up and go inside anyway.

The New World is as I remember it, small, intimate; the woodstove in the front corner by the window; people at small tables or booths partitioned off by weathered, rough-hewn doors. People talking quietly. People playing chess, a few look up when I enter but there is no recognition in their faces. I scan faces hoping to see Julian or any of the people I knew so well back then or anyone who might offer a friendly welcoming face but the last thing I did before leaving Illyria was claim my righteousness against their sin, my salvation against their damnation. Not in those words but pretty much.

I'll just sit at a booth away from the door maybe I will disappear, maybe I can sleep here. And again the music. I forgot how music fed me then. How it carried me. Leonard Cohen singing about Suzanne and I am transported back in time to a place both magical and threatening. And all those concerts. And the way it all spoke to the exact moments of my life. 'Here comes the Sun,' after my first winter in Illyria after months of overcast skies and exactly when the sun did begin to peek through. The exact moment.

Then there in a booth, all the way to the back, I see Lee siting alone writing. His back is turned but I recognize his shoulders, his long black hair, much longer now. Lee who I missed and thought of so often when I became a Christian. Lee who wrote such beautiful poetry, who I lived with off and on during that last winter before I left it all. We wrote in the spare bedroom of his brother's house in Springer. Just me and him sitting on a bare mattress in an otherwise bare room, passing the typewriter back and forth, collaborating on a strange and wandering play. Lee whose image rose up before me too often as I prayed, whose image became the image of Jesus as I prayed but who would not bow to Jesus. Such a conundrum.

Who one day just said I had to go.

He looks up when I sit down across from him at the booth, stops writing for just a moment. An almost imperceptible shiver runs through him then he returns to his writing.

"Nell. No, no, no . . . No," he says, using my street name, looking up again.

He returns to his writing.

A flood of insecurity washes over me, that same insecurity, that same Hell I thought I was saved from when I became a Christian. The New World suddenly shimmering and cloudy - both. I get up to leave but he takes hold of my hand, stops me, asks me to stay, says he's just shocked to see me is all.

The walls close in and the room tilts, I grab hold of the table to keep from falling.

"Breathe," he says. "You're white as a ghost."

I sit again, keep my eyes down, focus on my breath as he speaks softly. Words I can't understand but that remind me where I am, who I am. Lee gets up, orders tea for us. By the time he returns with the little tea pot and our cups I have settled again. But the realization that I could once again be faced with this time warped insecurity has sobered me and humbled me. My long days of Christianity didn't fix me at all, I only sidestepped the issue and now, once again it slams me in the face.

"You still Christian?" He asks. "You look different from when you used to show up preaching. I avoided you, you probably never saw me but I saw you out there handing out tracts, hounding people."

"I saw you. And I avoided you too, I was afraid that you would be a stumbling block and I was afraid of backsliding . . . of falling," I say when he looks puzzled at my ministry lingo.

"You still writing?" He asks.

"No. Not a word. Not a line. I tried many times. Kept trying but without success. Not since being out there, in the houses, out at Zion, in the Ministry," I say, stumbling over the words avoiding the word, the word - Christian. "There's this need to only praise and when I wrote it down it felt artificial.

"I've lived all this time as a servant of God - one of His sheep. This has been my goal. But now I've left and I'm marked: It's a way of protecting the rest of the sheep from the deceptions of the devil."

"Nell, Jesus fucking, do you even hear what you're saying? Do you hear the words? Words have meaning, have power. You are a wordsmith. Your poetry had promise, our play was maybe incoherent but so what? it showed we could produce and we could work together. Now I wonder if you even know what you're implying by the language you have become so accustomed to. Sheep? That was the goal? To become sheep?"

I try to hear his words but all I hear is my street name, Nell.

This name in my ears brings back those days, days consumed by the work, the spark of writing into the unknown. The feeling of being vitally alive. "You were never far from me the whole time," I say. "I can't explain it but I have to find my way back."

"Back?"

"Someone recently said I was in danger of losing my soul and now . . . I don't know how to find it back. It's not just words. I am the perfect sheep. I am the virtuous woman. That, not me. I am not me. Who I was. I can't feel who I am outside the one I tried so hard to become."

"Brainwashed."

"We said 'washed in His blood.'"

"I couldn't live like that."

We drink our tea in silence. Being in The New World is good, here is a thread to before I . . . annihilated myself. "Back before, somehow back before and work my way forward. I have to remember myself."

Lee understands perfectly. "Yes," he says. "Yes! And write it, go inside it. Don't write about it, write it. Remember our play?" he asks. "Write like that. Just write, don't reread, don't self censor. Be fearless."

Taking a deep breath I realize I've been holding it for years.

We sit a long time in silence. Lee puts his pens and paper in his backpack.

"I'm ready to go. If you need a place to stay you're welcome to crash at my place, stay in my back porch."

Lee's house feels familiar, old secondhand furniture like before and musical instruments in the corner. It feels homey. He asks if I want to get high.

"After living inside that straight jacket all these years seems like you could use a moment to just let down. And just be, just be. How long can you hold it together without exploding? Or imploding. So straight, so, so . . . straight."

The impulse to dive in, to release it all and just let go, is strong. Stronger is the fear of rebellion. Rebellion against Liam whose voice now whispers, 'I told you so.' His hold on us is tight because we believe our fall is inevitable outside the ministry. To leave the ministry means to fall. Means to plunge headlong - my exact impulse.

"No. Not tonight."

"How about a glass of wine then? This week I splurged and spent $19 on a good red from Napa Valley. 'Hints of chocolate and berries, oak tannins, ah.' The guy assured me it was good. Promise, no demands, no expectations. You really need to let down, Nell."

In my family we drank wine from teenage years. At the table. My dad traveled in Europe and brought the casual custom home. Wine carries none of the baggage that pot or LSD or any of the other drugs do.

"Wine then. But no sex. I'm not sleeping with you. I know the man code."

"The man code? You learn that in the cult?"

"No . . . that comes from the street. You know how it goes, glass of wine with a man - and especially at a man's home - means he thinks the woman wants sex, expects sex. No? And of course that means he expects . . . ."

"Okay, not going to put the moves on you tonight. You'll have a glass of wine then?"

The first sip spins into a whorl of sudden and unexpected elation. 'Letting down' as Lee said. Letting down after four years of straight jacket obedience to and to, and Lee now an old friend who I once loved, who I somehow saw in my prayer times. His dark skin, his long black hair his beauty and poetry. We danced then with words and mingled our bodies in druginduced bliss.

"Do you know who I am?" he asks.

Looking into his dark eyes, his darkness his sudden beauty I remember completely our times writing into the long nights. Our flight into a kind of madness only writing and writers can comprehend.

"I know you. I know you and remember us in our madness and in our beauty. We soared then as I have not soared since. But you are not IT, I want to find IT on my own. I can not depend on any man again. Do you understand?"

"Yes. It is good."

Lee puts on some Chet Baker and lights the fire and together we drink wine and remember who we were. Those days were not so easy. The demands of the drugs were not so easy. The ease of tonight feels like riding a soft current down a quiet river whereas beforetimes felt like unpredictable rapids. My mouth is a flood. I have held my tongue for so long I am afraid of myself but I can not stop. I tell Lee about my prayers when his face rose up before me. My Jesus who would not bow to Jesus. He listens quietly, saying nothing, allowing this flood to pour forth. It is a healing rain, an ambush of thoughts and emotion, a singular pain that I have held in for a very long time. I am glad he respects the threshold of my body, the decision to not have sex this night in my vulnerability.

"You laughed at me two nights ago," I say. "I heard you and saw you. You laughed at me because I was going to get married to a man who was proper and pedestrian and who I felt no love for but thought it was my righteous duty to marry for the sacrifice and spiritual grandeur of it."

"I'm glad I laughed. I would have laughed had I actually been there."

"It was like you were there all along. You were always there. Not so much you but . . . ."

"It's okay. I get it."

Wade

❖

Andrew is gone, Lily has disappeared. And the fire is going in summer.

Whispers, conspiratorial voices and sidewise looks and guilty guilty. Charlie avoids me, and the sisters look to themselves gossiping their ideas about what they heard or didn't hear. A wave of gossip. Voices unleashed in a dangerous freedom.

Liam waits in line for breakfast, only the second time since I've been here. Some act of clarification is in order before the flames of our tongues burn us all down. Surely he has something to say about the whole ghastly thing we witnessed and a scripture to go with it but so far he's just eating. Eyes focused too, too hard on the cornmeal mush in front of him. Charlie seated beside him stops talking and focuses on his mush too. Then the others at the table, then like a ripple outward the room becomes silent except for the sound of spoons clicking, and chewing.

Finally Liam stands and addresses the room. "Last night we witnessed something I hoped I'd never see. We watched one of our own fall into the hands of false doctrine. Seeing one of the our most fervent brothers fall, in a moment, in a heart beat, to one whose heart was bent to the will of the Deceiver was horrifying to us all, and it showed me how precious is our time here in these last days and how seriously we must take the scriptures that exhort us to be diligent about our salvation. Andrew will be alright. He'll go to one of the houses where he can heal."

The room is silent. Liam stands a long time without speaking. Looking around he begins again, his voice almost too quiet to hear, "I have something else to speak of to all of you. Last night made me realize that our time here is very short and that I can no longer put off something I've been wanting to share with all of you for a long time.

"We read in Matthew chapter 5, verses 31-32 *'It hath been said, Whosoever shall put away his wife, let him give her a writing of divorcement: But I say unto you, That whosoever shall put away his wife, saving for the cause of fornication, causeth her to commit adultery: and whosoever shall marry her that is divorced committeth adultery.'*

"This is very personal," he says, walking to the fireplace where he can see all of us. "I've come here to put myself in your hands. Jesus speaks of a man and a woman becoming one flesh. Then Jesus clearly states the exception, *'And I say to you, whoever divorces his wife, except for fornication, and marries another woman commits adultery.'*

"Cass left me, she has been found in the sin of fornication. She and Sawyer. It's been going on for quite a while now. The devil works against us in times of chaos, like last night. But now we must come together under one fellowship again and I need your blessing. I'm filing for divorce. And I want to remarry. I believe this scripture speaks to this exact situation. I trust the Lord and trust you all to either allow this or ask for my resignation as your pastor.

"I'm putting myself in your hands and I will let you decide. Whatever you decide in this matter I will receive without question. I want you to know that I am ready to step down as your pastor if any one of you and I mean that, just one of you, believes I am acting against scripture because it's my desire to remarry. I have asked our sister Emily to marry me and she has agreed."

This whiplash today, this morning, after Andrew lost his mind in his desire to walk in faith, blindly trusting the Lord. Andrew, who some considered the most fervent of us all, aside from Liam himself. As much as his dedication had begun to fester and stink in my opinion, he was more zealous than anyone I'd ever known.

Like reaching down into the depth of our faith to revive something other than the afterimage of last night, Liam asks us to consider the future of our ministry. Liam's fate and our fate, will be decided. And Andrew's melt down is sidestepped. Forgotten? How short our memories are. And somehow Cass' sin has washed us all clean.

"It's Cass's fault if the ministry shuts down," Paul says on the way out to work in the garden. He stops, looks to me for agreement.

"The woman is the weaker vessel," Charlie says, rubbing his hands together, groveling for approval. "It's why they need us to guide them, to be the head. Poor Liam, he must be hurting. The women must be held to account for their sin. Cass was a stumbling block from the beginning. We all knew she still smoked, in the bathroom to hide, but you could smell it on her. She was caught up in a false doctrine and this is where it led. Off by a millimeter today, off by a million miles tomorrow, that's what Liam always says. The trajectory doesn't lie. And the sickness came through last winter? That was God's way of rebuke for tolerating sin in the camp. The Children of Israel knew the reward for sin when even one of them strayed or acted out. Cass brought sickness but now with her gone we can heal."

Liam walks by on his way to the trailer, head down, eyes to the ground. I've never seen this side of him. He seems more ... human?

"He's broken," I say. "If he weren't so humbled there's no way I'd go along with granting him this . . . grace? Old Testament times, he'd get no slack. We live more Old Testament than New.

There's no grace, not really. Not for us. '*If a man does not work neither shall he eat.*' That's what we hear everyday. It's drilled into us that faith without works is dead and . . . and . . . I don't like it."

"Will you object then? Go against the scriptures?" Paul asks. "Will you be the one to break us all apart? My guess is that if he goes the whole thing goes."

"No. But it's because I believe we are God's chosen. Is it Liam that holds it together? He did bring us together with his visions and his relationship with the Lord. I do believe that but not that he holds us together. And even if he does then it's because it's God put him here for that purpose. What does that mean anyway? Liam stepping down. But no, I'm not going to object."

"Wait up," Marty calls out.

"You working in the garden today?" I ask.

"Yeah, I don't have a permanent stewardship yet so I thought it'd be good to work outside with you guys."

"You have an opinion about Liam?" Paul asks in that same casual way we say 'how're you doing?' not expecting any response other than 'fine,' and in this case not expecting any answer other than, 'no opinion here.'"

Marty's hands slowly clinch into fists, he looks to the woods and frowns, unwilling to say anything. Mostly young converts go along with whatever is happening but something about Marty's reaction says otherwise. I can actually feel his struggle, that need to say what is expected that battles against what you really think.

"Marty," I say, "what do you really think?"

"That Cass and Sawyer aren't together."

His voice is just above a whisper then he holds silence.

Paul is adamant, demanding to know why and on what grounds he can say such a thing, in essence accusing Liam of lying. It's never been done. But Marty won't say.

"Liam is God's anointed and God's anointed doesn't lie," Charlie says over his shoulder on his way to the garden. Paul too leaves, disgusted.

"Can you tell me what's going on, Marty? Just between us?"

"Is anything ever just between us?"

It's true, I never intended what he said to remain just between us. My own words condemn me.

"If I tell you, do you promise before the Lord that you will keep it to yourself?"

"Okay, I promise. But you must know that if you stand against Liam's divorce and remarriage you'll be expected to give an explanation. Before the whole body. Not just us here at Zion, it will be something everyone in the houses will need to know."

"I haven't decided to tell anyone or to stand against Liam. How can I? Who am I? I've been a Christian and in the ministry less than four months."

"So what's your objection. On what grounds can you say Liam lied?"

"Sawyer's gay. He doesn't go with women, never has. We spent that time up on the mountain and I saw who Sawyer is, really is. He's different than who he is here among the brethren. When it got cold we had to get right up inside that elk. We had to hold close to keep from freezing. Sawyer held me with a tenderness and kindness I've only experienced with girls. He wasn't afraid to be close enough to protect me from the freeze like you'd expect from a guy. He didn't try anything but eventually he confessed to me. He kinda had to since he got hard and kinda had to say something. I don't have a problem with it," Marty says, "but here in the ministry I think it would be a big problem and it's not my place to share that but now with Liam saying him and Cass? It's not possible. You get it don't you? So now you know. Sorry, maybe by speaking, I put something into your hands that you shouldn't have to carry."

"Wow. I don't know what to say to that. How do you know he didn't get hard for any number of reasons. Being gay being just one."

"We talked. I just said that."

"Hmm. I can't say anything I don't know first hand. I believe you think you know what you know but I can't act on that."

Marty

❖

Hearing Liam accuse Sawyer and Cass in front of the brethren, hearing Liam lie. Watching his face - a mask of humility, a lyingmask, a fake. Sawyer was a friend a better friend than I've known in a very long time, or maybe ever, especially here. Tracking, walking the path, the trees the bushes the sliding granite slabs leading down into berrypatches and azaleas. Ferns and mushrooms beside the trail and then the spot of blood I saw and the encouragement to keep trying, to keep looking, to keep trying to follow the path to where it led. Sawyer with his West Virginia talk colored with cussing, his acknowledgement of the violence of the hunt, of the sacred sacrifice of the animals. His determination to not leave an injured animal . . . Nothing in my past even comes close to his mind his heart his solid down to earth connection to survival and and

    better that Wade knows too, now not just in my hands

        even if Wade can't speak

  not just my decision.

Julian

❖

I meet Cass early at the Odyssey, a coffee house on University. The place is way too noisy so we walk the downtown streets toward the river. The cottonwoods grow tall and strong down here and the day is warm so we work our way down toward the water in silence each with our own thoughts.

The river burbles softly as we approach. Moving toward the sound we round a bend and there beside the trail stands a cottonwood larger than any I've ever seen before. We call these sacred trees warriors and this ancient relative speaks, like all cottonwoods, in the language of water. The gentle movement of its leaves mirrors the sound of water flowing gently within the banks of the river. Stillness and vibrancy surrounds this grandfather, both. I am overwhelmed. Cass tells me this is where she has come to pray all these years since they moved the ministry North.

She pulls out her cigarettes, takes out two, offers one to me. I rub the cigarette between my fingers to loosen the cánlí into my palm, I kneel down and place a pinch at the base of this Tunkasila on the side that faces the west direction, speaking words of reverence for this ancient tree, this Grandfather. Then moving sun-wise to the north direction, another pinch of tobacco. A flood of memories moves through me, memories of the buffalo nation and the Plains where I lived as a boy and of my father, his compassion his great love for me, his understanding way with me. As my connection to this ancient one and my ancestors strengthens, my connection to Uncí Makáh and especially the Tatanka nation strengthens. Then another prayer to the east. As I move, as I make my prayer in each direction, I find myself rising until I am standing, my forehead pressing into the trunk, arms outstretched around this massive trunk. Finally, I offer what remains of the tobacco to the south direction and step back.

Cass follows, making her own prayers to the four directions and when she comes to the south direction she lifts her hand and the Canlí to the sky, to Skan, and then stoops to touch the earth with the last of the tobacco and speaks softly to our Grandmother, Uncí Makáh. Backing up she stands beside me and begins a prayer song to this warrior before us. Then we follow the trail down to the river and sit quietly.

"It's good to remember the ways, to speak the language. I'm glad we met," I say.

"Liam made up some story about me and then kicked me out. He's keeping the kids away from me. He's got an expensive lawyer," Cass says.

"Whoa, that heartless bastard. I didn't like the vibe out there but that's way beyond what I imagined, coming from a Christian. If you need anything, a place to stay . . . I have a friend, Lee, a Diné brother, who'd let you crash . . . ."

"It's not that, it's just . . . . I can't believe he actually did it. He's threatened this over the years, ever since he started inviting street people to live in our house and I objected. Ever since I didn't go along with his 'revelations' about the Bible. And the stories he's telling people about me - adultery is probably just the beginning. I'm sure he'll tell my children that stuff too. It's his way to set the narrative. Especially now that I'm gone. His reality is that if you leave you'll immediately backslide, fall into drugs or false doctrine. In his universe there's no other possible outcome, and no other way to serve God than what he believes, what he teaches. And they all live in that expectation of their fate; that they're lost to God and to themselves if they ever leave or do something to warrant being marked. It's totally unconscious and that's what makes it so powerful."

We sit a long time in silence, listening to the voice of the river and the cottonwood leaves rustling. The comforting sounds of our warrior brother, the tree of life.

"And it won't occur to anyone out there that I deserve my own children. People have been taking n'dn children from their parents far too long - feels like historical trauma repeating itself."

"I'll be taking off soon," I say. "To South Dakota, finish my dance. It's a strong ceremony on Pine Ridge. Join me. It would be good for you. I want to get there early enough to do a Hanbléca, and go through purification. Plus I need to get clear of Illyria."

"I'll make some prayers, offer up some tobacco, see if any dreams come. It would be good to stand in the circle with you but I can't say yet. We need to take the Inipi down, though. I know it would be better for us to just keep on using it while you're still here but the way things are coming apart out there I would guess some people might find more freedom to actually take a walk and explore the forest and then end up finding it. I want us to get one more sweat in first, then take it down. It would be a bitter fight if we tried to keep it going."

"It needs to come down in a good way," I say. "Take care of the prayers and the spirits that took care of us, move the stone people back to where they came from, so they can return to their own. You say it's coming apart out there?"

"Just a hunch. Obviously it seems like it to me but I think others will be noticing Liam's erratic behavior before too long."

"Then let's plan a lodge this week. My friend Lee, the Diné brother, wants to join us. Is there a way to contact Lily?"

"Next couple of days then. Not sure how to get through to Lily. Everything happened so fast. Last night Andrew lost his mind then Lily disappeared then Liam made his announcement."

"Lily disappeared? That mean she didn't marry Andrew?"

"No. She didn't. And she just left, no word, no nothing."

"Maybe she's in town. I'll start looking for her and I'll talk to Lee, see if he wants to join us for this lodge, I'll let him know. I'm staying there off and on these days until I take off."

PART III

Liam

❖

The book of Revelations. The apostle John, alone on the isle of Patmos, the island of his exile, full of visions and the voice of the Lord speaking in his hearing. The voice of God speaking and guiding his words and writings. John hearing, then setting down the words for each of us to ponder, to learn from. 'He who has ears to hear let him hear.'

"Like John, moment by moment we live by faith. The book of Acts teaches us how we must live. And that is how we live. What we are witness to is the direct line from the Old Testament kings and prophets to us, and a direct line from Christ's apostles to us. We are of the lineage of Abraham, Isaac and Jacob and of those first Christians who knew Jesus. We are the lineage of those who through faith subdued kingdoms and wrought righteousness."

Marty

❖

Nothing. no mention. not even the chance for anyone else's voice. But what did I expect? Charlie and Paul together nodding, singing, hands raised in praise. Cass is gone, kicked out of Zion, marked. Wade's hard to read, relieved? Shut down? Easier to just keep things the same? I can't. The curtain is pulled back and I can't. My own version of Oz, of wizardry, but where to now? Not good enough to stay for the safety of it the future of it the way of life the comfort and friendships living without the struggle the emptiness the blank page staring me down that is my life Too much time a forward future place undefined and with no direction or sense of a path forward this trail goes on and on and on there are no footprints to follow this is what untethered feels like after the swarm of the hive mind the ease of living in the knowledge of future times and the end of days all spelled out all explained guided and blessed always in the knowledge that it is above all God's Will the ultimate congrat the final A+ the father the teacher the elder the God all approve all at once such is this place of peace.

I can't

After the study Liam calls me out, takes me aside, quietly lets me know I'm being moved. Tonight. "Get your things together, you're moving to town. Meet me at the car in twenty minutes."

"Now?"

"Are you questioning God?" he rebukes. "Be instant in season and out of season. Twenty minutes. And don't talk to anyone about this. Do you understand?"

I only have my sleeping bag and a change of clothes, my guitar. A minute ago I was thinking to go now I'm afraid to leave. The house in town might be easier. Might even run into Sawyer. He's not marked to me.

"What are you doing?" Charlie asks when he sees me rolling up sleeping bag, packing up my stuff.

"I'm moving to town, to the 10th Street house. Oh wait, Liam said not to mention it to anyone so don't say nothing, okay?"

"Okay, wonder why he wants it kept quiet."

"I don't know just . . . don't say nothing."

I walk out toward the pasture one last time look around to remember in case this is the last time. The horses are out watching me. Inside the barn is some hay so I feed them for a while.

Liam finds me there and rebukes me for wasting his time looking for me.

"The van is warmed up and ready. Are you ready?"

"Yes," I say.

"Move then, the van is ready."

The van is hot and steamy after the cool chill of the night and the walk back from the barn. The drive silent. Often when we are alone in the van, Liam says strange things. I've always thought of these odd sayings as a kind of Zen koan with a meaning behind the actual words that I've yet to discover. Tonight he's quiet and says nothing the whole time until we stop in front of the 10th Street house.

"You know what they say about power?" he asks suddenly. "They say power corrupts and absolute power corrupts absolutely."

Then he laughs, waits for me to get out of the van and drives off quickly. He's gone without a goodbye, God bless, or prayer. Our tradition is strong around new arrivals. If someone is driving them in they stay for Bible study or tea or at least just a greeting.

When I try the the door it's locked and when I knock no one answers. The light in the front room turns off while I'm standing there and now I'm looking at darkened windows and closed blinds. I can hear movement inside but no one will answer the door.

"It's me, it's Marty! I shout through the window. "Liam just dropped me off, let me in."

No one answers and after about fifteen minutes, I realize that no one is going to answer. The whole of it gradually sinks in that I've been kicked out of the ministry. Marked. Maybe because I talked to Wade? Maybe Liam knew about Sawyer?

I sit on the curb, wait. Maybe someone will come out. Maybe it was a mistake. Maybe I'm dreaming. Nothing seems real.

Maybe Liam didn't really mean to do this. There must be some mistake. I go back, try the door again and again I knock until someone comes out, a brother I've never seen before. He tells me to go away that they aren't allowed to talk to me. So it's true. I'm marked.

Julian

❖

Lee sits outside the New World at a small table drinking coffee, seeing me he goes inside, orders me a coffee. "Good to see you again," he says. "Davis came by a while ago. Hadn't seen him for months, said you'd gone out with him to that Christian place and did some tracking on the horses a while back. Must have been nice to get back with the horse nation."

"Yeah, that was a while ago. I had no idea it would affect me the way it did. Brought a lot of things up, a flood pouring back. Dreams mostly but waking times too. The bear's come out of hibernation and is reminding me of my vow."

"Your vow?"

"Yeah, my ceremony. It got cut short when I got drafted; then I came here, stayed drunk. Couldn't go back. This whole time there's been this feeling I couldn't shake, sense of necessity, to stay here. I didn't question or know why I just stayed, but now it's gone.

"Some time after or during our Inipi it lifted. Inipi with Cass and then with Cass and Lily, the one who took care of the horses and then it was gone. Just like that and then I remembered my vows. Remembered who I was, who I am.

"Maybe staying was about me or maybe it was about Lily too. We cooked her up real good in the lodge. Real nice lodge. Hot lodge. Very sacred. I trust the ceremony to do its work. And have to leave it there. But now I have to finish my prayers."

"In South Dakota? You dance?"

"Yeah, back to South Dakota, finish my vow. My uncle's been waiting patiently these years since Nam, letting me cool off after and now it's time. The Red Road's calling me back home. Sounds easy after this winter."

Lee nods, sips his coffee.

"This whole time in Illyria, fighting against something I couldn't name. And this town seemed the right place for a good fight. Inside fight, pitting myself against wanting anything to do with my traditions. Nam mostly broke me but I'd never admit it. We been sweating all this month. The lodge is out on some forest land near where Davis took me. Good strong ceremonies with Cass, the Lakota woman who's married to the fearless leader of the whole shebang. First time I felt at home in a long time was inside that lodge. First time my head cleared. But it wasn't until we sweated out Lily that it completely shifted. That pressure to stay in Illyria that still lingered finally vanished. Finally let up and now I'm ready to go. Face the rez again. Face it down by fulfilling my vows."

"How many years you got left?"

"Two, but I want to keep dancing. It's a good life that way. Walking the Red Road. Better than walking the Milky Way."

"True that. When're you leaving?"

The sun touches the horizon, flashes through the clouds then the sky turns deep red. We watch a long time in silence.

"I'll be around for a while," I say.

"Saw Cass today, the Lakota woman you're talking about, she invited me out to sweat with you guys tomorrow. To the lodge you're talking about. You need a ride?"

"Thanks, yeah."

"You need anything, you know. To help get you ready or anything, just let me know."

"I need to sweat. Purify like my life depends on it, which it does. It'll be good to have you in the Inipi with us."

Wade

❖

Working with Charlie in the morning, finish work on the brother's dorm going slowly then in the crowded dining hall during lunch Liam comes in, announces that Marty left during the night, that we are to have no communication with him. That he is marked. Just that, short to the point.

Liam's face's a distortion, an unsuccessful mask, an attempt to undo the smile that can't undo itself? In an attempt to appear humble, pride bleeds through. A victory? A final blow to anything that might threaten him? Little Marty?

"I knew something was up with Marty." Charlie says after we return to work. "He lied to me the other night when he ran off. He said he was being moved to the house in town. It only now makes sense. I guess I'm glad Cass left though. She was a stumbling block. Seems like a lot of people though. Sawyer, Cass, Lily, Marty, not to mention Andrew. And Lily just up and left. What was up with Lily?"

"I thought you heard. I thought everyone heard. Andrew tried to rape her. Some scripture running through his head over and over about David and Bathsheba and he thought it was the Lord."

"Geeez, that's messed up. Anyone talk to Lily?"

"No one saw her go. Andrew told me about it. He blamed her for hurting his nose when she got away from him. Such a baby."

"Geeez."

"Does Liam seem off to you lately?" I ask.

"He's carrying a heavy load for the Lord. His burden is much heavier than ours. Then his wife runs off with Sawyer. Anyone'd be stunned and shaken. He's a Saint of the Lord and anointed but he still feels things."

"But about Sawyer, I don't think Cass ran off with him."

"Of course she did. You think Liam's lying? What're you implying?"

"Nothing, it's just that . . . Oh, never mind."

"Well watch your words, hold your tongue."

Charlie's sudden aggression sets me aback.

"I speak for your edification, brother. "*Whoso keepeth his mouth and his tongue keepeth his soul from troubles.* Proverbs 21:23 Liam has me memorize certain scriptures, I say this for your edification brother, not to condemn. Amen?"

"Aaah," I wave him off, leave the table to play the piano before we return to work. First Andrew goes off the rails, then these three leave. This hasn't happened before. If it was at one of the houses the pastor would be brought back to Zion. Four people in as many days? Three in one night

"*Even so the tongue is a little member, and boasteth great things. Behold, how great a matter a little fire kindleth!* James 3:5." Charlie talking from the table half way across the dining hall.

The rest of the afternoon Charlie looks at me as though I'm a stranger and eventually turns his back on me and works in stubborn silence.

Sawyer.
Marty.
Cass.
Lily.

Marty

❖

If it hadn't been forced on me would I have had the courage to leave? Would I have ever left? Ever? Even after Liam's dishonesty and silence I didn't. I couldn't.

Out on the street just two blocks from my parents' house and I felt completely lost. But they welcomed me with tears of joy. My mom so glad to hear from me again, after almost four months of not knowing, she almost broke down with worry. This is what I did in my grand elevation to sainthood, to salvation, not thinking at all about them. Thinking only of myself. My dad so open to my return, granting instant forgiveness. The prodigal son in reverse yet it crushed them all the same. My home, my warm, clean bed, the healing cocoa from the cupboard, my happy little sister who thought I'd gone to our cousin's house in California for the time.

Is the ministry, bigger than the last 24 hours? Is it really the fellowship of the saints except for this awful twisted moment? God's children, walking in the Lord, upright in the faith - actually living the Word of God like Liam says, except for this little, this one, moment? Or is this contradiction who we are? This sham?

Even cast out, Jesus is inside. Liam can't take that from me. And my Bible, I have that and I can hear the words for myself now. And not feel like I have to change them to fit Liam's interpretation, our interpretation. The ministry's interpretation.

There is a freedom in that and oddly, excitement. Excitement to reread and hear for myself. The word of God to guide. Liam's a man, the ministry is faulty. Maybe. Maybe not. But this is my walk in the spirit, my cross to bear and I will keep my heart toward Jesus soft and open. Liam can't take that away.

Walking aimlessly in the warm morning sun, an old habit in this town, I end up across the street from the 10th Street house. One of the brothers is clipping hedges. I've never seen him before, he doesn't know me.

"Good morning," I say, crossing the street.

"Good morning," he says. "Have you heard the Good News about Jesus?"

Can I pull this trigger? Can I speak truth? Speak against Liam? Criticize Liam? No.

"I have," I say. "Just came by to say hi."

"Praise the Lord. Come in and I'll introduce you to the brethren."

"No, not now, maybe come back later."

"But why not? A few brothers and some sisters are inside who'd love to meet you. Most are at work. Have you eaten, I can get some breakfast together?"

"I'm good, thanks though," I say before continuing down the tree lined street.

Even that, just that contact felt good. But no, I won't go back, not ever.

Paul

❖

The five of us already in the room sit around a long table. We've been waiting a half hour and are ready to get on with it. The work of the Lord isn't about waiting it's about doing and this sitting, this waiting grates.

"Just say it, Jacob. There's no way around it but to just spit it out," Josh says when they finally arrive, locking the door behind them.

"Where's Liam?" I ask. "An elder's meeting without Liam? What's up?"

Jacob stands, eyes steady, glaring at me, holding the silence, one finger tapping the table, the only sound in the room. Then his expression softens. "You know what Liam said about Cass and Sawyer?" he asks, looking around the room at each of us. "Well I know for a fact that none of it is true. Not a word of it."

Jacob is one of four elders in the hierarchy, immediately below Liam and today these two, Jacob and Josh, are here at Zion just for this meeting. We were called at the last minute and weren't told anything. Now I know why, this blasphemy could only happen under the cover of darkness. I never fully trusted Jacob, he struck me as too straight, too clean cut, too businessman-in-a-suit. And here he stands accusing Liam, God's anointed, sent to guide us in these last days. Liam the one who hears the voice of the Lord clearly and has the courage of his faith to act on what the Lord reveals.

Jacob was never on the road, he came to the ministry in the early days straight laced and is all business - always. Among us he is one of only a few who wear pressed, button down shirts and slacks. No flannel, no army surplus, no boots. He works in an office and lives in town on his own and not in one of the houses. He's clean shaven, wears his hair short, an outsider among outsiders. His Bible studies are good but coming from a decidedly different, even opposite position from Liam's studies. And maybe that's the root of this accusation. His vision of our ministry is a place where the men prepare for life outside the ministry. Concerning the women there is no difference, they are always looked on as helpmates to a man's ministry. Liam's vision sees us inside this safe and spiritually superior place forever: A continuation of the disciples' lives as expressed in the second chapter of Acts, where we hold all things in common, own nothing and trust the Lord for everything. And I've always agreed. If we are walking this way in accordance with scriptures and in direct relation with the Lord then why change that? Now as I listen to his accusation I think he must be angling for Liam's position. I've never trusted Jacob and I think he knows it.

Standing, I prepare to leave. "This is anathema and blasphemy. I can't sit here and listen to it."

"Wait," Josh says quietly, "hear us out."

If it wasn't for Josh I would have bolted but Josh is a good guy, has always been humble. Fred and Greg also stand, objecting to Jacob but Josh calls on all of us to hear them out.

"Just by hearing this I am convicted of sin," Greg says. "To take this in, to allow it to sit in my heart without rejection reeks of sin."

"Just hear us out," Josh repeats. "We know it's hard to hear but this is important enough for us to to have traveled from out of state to bring you together to counsel with us on what we've learned and what we believe needs to happen. The other elders are in agreement, now it's up to you to hear us out."

"Cass has not been with Sawyer," Jacob says. "Josh and I both know that as a fact."

"How could you know such a thing," Fred shouts, leaning into Jacob, towering over Jacob, a threatening gesture even without his raised voice.

"Back off," Jacob shouts back, always confrontational, always confident in himself that he is in the right, always ready to fight. "Josh and I are your elders and have a responsibility to inform not only you all but all the brethren as well. The scriptures are clear about elders. Their walk must be blameless, their house in order. We know this story about Sawyer and Cass is a lie because Sawyer is gay. He's been open with us, Josh and I. He knows it's only sin if he acts on it."

"Marty was aware of this. Liam told him he was being moved to the house in Illyria but the pastor was told he was marked and not to let him in," Josh says. "Marty was silenced, had to be, because his knowledge was a threat. Liam never knew that Sawyer had come out to us. We never mentioned it."

Fred sinks down in the chair followed by me and then Greg.

What cowards we are. These two speak and we attack or want to run. But the words confirm fleeting thoughts and impressions I've shut out for a long while. Questions I refused to ask about Sawyer, concerns I rejected about Liam's odd behavior, all shoved down into oblivion. How easy *that* is, it's second nature anymore. Easier not to think.

And I was the one Liam used to send Sawyer away, so proud to be Liam's helper in that moment, thinking I'm moving up in the ministry thinking maybe eventually to sit with these elders on their level. The easy cruelty of it as I looked down on his disobedience, never believing there could be any response to Liam other than absolute trust, absolute obedience.

"There are other things. This is just the tip of the iceberg," Jacob says. "Liam's been spending ministry funds, funds that come from the houses, from the labors of the brothers and sisters who eat beans and corn meal mush and have to ration toilet paper. He's spending it on himself, on his fancy champion bloodline, registered Russian Wolfhounds, on the new home he just purchased on thirty acres and the motor home he just bought to tour the houses. It's been going on a long time, started with the horses and grew from there. Always justified somehow. We thought we were learning to ride the horses because the world was running out of gas and we'd be prepared, know how to ride and keep and train horses so we could continue the work of the Lord. But now, looking at all of it, it comes clear it's not from the Lord. And he's been in the planing stages these past months, preparing a trip to all the houses to establish a kingdom unto himself - remove us, separate himself from his elder down south, remove all authority but his own.

"We've been praying about this, Josh and I, and we plan to go to him, ask him to repent. Repent or leave."

"What makes you think he'll listen to you?" I ask. "What makes you think anyone will listen to you for that matter. His is the only voice the brethren have ever heard. Your words will mean nothing. Less than nothing if Liam refuses to repent and everyone continues to follow him. You'll be, we'll be, the ones leaving. Or repenting."

"Have any of you thought Liam's behavior's been off lately?" Jacob asks.

Hesitant nods.

"But not until just now did it come into focus. Like puzzle pieces falling into place with a loud click!" Fred says, his anger now turned toward Liam.

"And have any of you heard anything, any gossip or anything of criticism around Liam's behavior lately? Or ever for that matter?"

"Never. Not possible." I say.

"It's what we thought," Jacob says. "We believe there are probably many who thought something wasn't right but no one has been able to believe it or even clearly see it much less voice it. Until today - in this room. Josh and I only began talking together and to the other elders after Liam announced that

Sawyer and Cass were in a relationship. Liam used Cass as a scapegoat and used Sawyer to prove the point of infidelity because Liam had moved on and was ready to have a new helpmate, Emily, who would fully support him. We put it together that Liam had kicked Sawyer out to set it up so he could divorce Cass because of infidelity and remarry. It had to be done that way because of our reliance on scripture. He kind of boxed himself in and had to get out in a way that was consistent with scripture.

"Liam's vision to go to all the houses didn't strike us as at the time But then we learned that he planned to get a commitment from everyone in the ministry to his authority alone. We don't know that this was going to be stated but it was the point. To build a kingdom unto himself, it's what we eventually discovered. At first we tried to justify it because of the strength of Liam's relationship to the Lord and the miraculous way things just happened in his presence. But it was in conflict with everything we, as elders, lived by - our reliance on the scriptures and how easy it is to be led astray by false doctrine.

"If you could see through our eyes, see what we've seen . . . it's obvious why everyone, we, even Liam needs an overseer, an elder. There were so many times we'd talked about the lack of an elder as the seed, and heresy the fruit. This was where the notion of off by and inch today is off by a thousand miles tomorrow began. This was a point of departure we couldn't watch without doing something.

"But only when this business with Cass came up did Josh and I talk together and then decide to say something to you all. As your elders we couldn't remain silent with this knowledge, it's too much of a threat to everything we believe . . . . This is not easy for any of us but it had to be brought into the light."

"So are we in agreement that something has to be done, that we need to act, to confront Liam, to clear this up?" Josh asks.

Again nods but this time without hesitation.

"Then we proceed."

"So how to do this?" Jacob asks, speaking the question in all our minds. "This is why we called all of you together. This is a time to hear everyone's thoughts. We agree on what has to be done, confront him, but the how and the when remain a question."

I remember hearing a pastor in one of the houses ask someone what they wanted to do. Not, 'this is what God has told me you should do,' but 'what do you want to do.' The question dumfounded me. I thought about that a long time because in our ministry I have learned not to do what I want to do, not to think what I want to think but to yield and let God guide, and mostly do what I'm told. Now asked what I think we should do I can't think at all.

"We want to hear from you," Josh says. "What I'm thinking is talk to Liam, confront him on his sin, ask him to repent - to recommit to the Lord and to the ministry, to humble himself. Seek counsel from us and his elder in the south or leave, see how he takes it."

"Then what?" I ask.

"If he repents it ends there," Fred says.

"I'm thinking we need to talk to the brethren first," Jacob says. "Let them know Liam's in sin and what we are going to ask him to do. Then talk to Liam."

"I disagree, why talk to the brethren first?" Josh asks

"Because once Liam knows what we're up to, and if he's not willing to repent, he'll gather together as many of the brethren as he can, turn them against us, tell a story of his victimhood. Twist it. Say he's being persecuted for his greater faith. That we are jealous or something."

"No, we have to talk to Liam first. We won't even know if he will agree to repent until we confront him. It would be the worst kind of backbiting," Josh says. "It will come off as backbiting too. We can't call him on his sin in a way that is not perfect in the sight of the Lord. Otherwise we're no better than he is."

The freedom to think and wrangle a question like this feels like drunkenness. The freedom to speak our minds reeks of sin.

"What's God's will in this?" I ask.

"Josh and I have prayed over this. We've spent long hours individually and together before the Lord and in Scriptures. We believe this is of the Lord or we wouldn't have come to you. It's the details we want to get clear today. But this needs to happen quickly, immediately after this meeting."

"I still say we talk to Liam first," Josh says. "If he refuses to repent, we call all the houses and the married couples, speak to everyone today, I've made lists, this needs to happen now. I say talk to him, hear him out. In the event he refuses to hear us out - refuses to admit his sin - we start making phone calls to everyone. Just do it, short conversations, let everyone know that we talked to Liam and what we confronted him with. Be clear. It all has to happen quickly because we believe he'll start making his own phone calls."

"If he won't repent do you think the ministry will continue?" I ask.

"Absolutely," Jacob says. "We'll call a Pastors' meeting two weeks out from today while we're on the phone with the pastors. That'll give them time to get out here and then we'll hash it all out. Of course it will continue, *Oh ye of little faith*, things will change though, things will definitely get better for the brethren in the houses and out here at Zion. We'll make sure of that."

Walking out of that meeting was like a dream inside a dream. Suddenly Liam was no longer infallible. Suddenly he was a used car salesman from New Jersey, the big secret he tried to keep from us but somehow suspected. Suddenly he was a bully and I wanted nothing more to do with him. My hope was that he would repent and that we could all forget about this but I doubted I would ever see him again as anything other than a shyster. The veil has lifted and the aura he carried is gone.

Lee

❖

The enclosed back porch is a snug harbor, has been for any who needed one, a mattress on the floor and a space heater. Nell's safe place for now. Two nights and she's still back there - not ready to come out.

Julian comes by, says we need to head out. The stones will be ready by the time we get there.

"Get your stuff ready," he says. "We'll leave as soon as you're ready to go."

I tell him there's an old friend out in the back porch. "Haven't seen her for almost four years. She said she was living out at that place you visited, Zion. Just out of the blue she walks off and leaves it behind. Then she shows up in town. I'm in the New World sitting in the back at one of the booths and there she is, sits down right in front of me. Fresh off the funny farm. Name's Nell," I say.

"Maybe she knows Lily. I need to contact Lily, let her know we're having a lodge today."

"I can ask her, seems like she might."

"That place is scary as shit, is what it is."

"Brainwashed and isolated. It's kind of a miracle Nell was able to leave. The things she says without even realizing how crazy. It's all normal out there for them but out here the contrast is crazy shit."

"Lily said the ministry, Zion and the houses too, provide a life apart where they can focus on their spiritual life and prayers without temptation. Made it sound good but she was not convincing. I could tell she was being crushed out there."

"Sounds like Nell. She said someone recently told her she was in danger of losing her soul. It shifted her in some way so at least she's got that to help her now she's away from that place. Said she wants to find her way back, write her way back. It's a long way back if you ask me."

"No way," Julian says on his way to the back porch. "It's Lily, it's got to be Lily. Her name's Lily."

Nell sits on the mattress on the floor, staring past her unopened Bible.

Julian stoops down, "Lily! Wow you got out . . . Lily . . . Lily, it me, it's Julian." But Lily doesn't even look up. Then real quiet, like he's talking to a wounded animal, a wild wounded animal likely to run off or fly away, "we're going out to the Inipi today, have ceremony again. Cass will be there, Lee's coming."

She looks at Julian then at me, a moment later she looks down at her unopened Bible. "I heard you two talking," she says, still looking at the Bible. "I want to go."

But she doesn't move and she doesn't look up again.

"Here, let me help you," Julian says.

"I'm okay, it's just strange, disorienting being outside the ministry. Being on my own again. I'm dizzy, feel like I'm in a time warp. I don't know if I like it. There was always a comfort in knowing I was always doing exactly the right thing, was always in exactly the right place. Now . . . it's too open, nothing but open space. Like I might fly out in all directions, atoms dispersing."

Julian gently offers to help her up. She resists help then lets herself be moved around. Julian looks to me but I'm no help at all. This is not something I've seen before, not even in bad LSD trips. But I can see she's in there. Holding on by a thread.

"Ceremony will help," I say finally. "I'll be ready in a minute. Get her out to my car and I'll be there in a minute."

"Bring stuff for her - a towel, something she can change into after," Julian calls back.

The drive out to the lodge is quiet. Nell, or Lily has not spoken since those few words in the porch. She just looks out the window. Julian guides us to a dirt road, says they rode the horses along there last winter.

The smell of smoke drifts through the open window. Healing fire, healing smoke.

Lily

❖

Coals and red stones and flicking flames inside a crescent of small rocks. inside the lodge it's dark and quiet that's my place now in darkness in heat and flame of fire what it means to hold onto nothing to have nothing to believe nothing to float without anchor I need the inside of the lodge so I wont float away crawl hands and knees all by myself the far edge away from the doorway away from the light this darkness is my darkness inky black like the goo inside same to same. Julian looks in sees my eyes smile sees my eyes my heart in his eyes looks back Cass looks in sees my heart Lee looks in, who is Lee who am I inside a dark place? quietly they crawl in mitakuyas, mitakuyas, Lee brings stone people to the doorway in they come one by one to the center the center holds the glowing. Stone people pulsate more and more they all come in tall pile a mountain glowing red and searing. Julian and Cass bring the bucket in cross the line of the little pit the stones live inside mitakuyas, mitakuyas. Lee crawls in mitakuyas the door open Cass sings Julian sings Lee sings my voice wont open to me not with the open door not with the light shining too too bright. Close the door I hear my voice say and the door flap folds down and takes away the light. now singing I sing we sing song after song heat searing my towel a little tent I live inside a womb inside a tent inside inside searing heat rain drops fall from the blankets overhead steam rising raining inside mitakuyas mitakuyas and bright light shines eyes hurt heart shuts the water bucket goes out touches the altar comes back darkness again again I breathe

no one can see me here this darkness is complete this is where I will live a tiny place a healing place Cass sings pure notes alone her song is for listening we listen there are no words to understand the beauty of not knowing not trying of only being wanting to stay here forever my home now this small hot place mitakuyas, mitakuyas and the flap opens cool air pours in with the light the light now not so scary the ground holds me up now my hands caress the soft earth and find cool moisture beneath the surface just beneath. Julian talking about tobacco says Canlí Lakota given to two leggeds for bridge to the sacred for offerings to plant nation and medicines and stone people and ancestor spirits to road kill to to to the dead bird along the trail and to sun and moon Wi and Hanwí they have names, Mní Wakan, water, has a name they are relatives my relatives the breathing earth is full of relatives before there was any other thing, or any time, Inyan was, and his spirit was Wakan - stone people, called Inyan were my first relative the first that I felt that time beside the fire Inyan who I offered tobacco to. Cass all this time refusing to give up Canlí our relative who bridges the gap Makáh too she has a name our mother earth I will learn language just words no ideas only words names no prayers only songs songs are prayers Lee knows he always knew why no mention? we wrote strange things strange magical things titled 'in the beginning was the word' and I never understood what that meant I never knew the beginnings of bible words then - Inyan, I hear my self saying - in the beginning was Inyan Lee crawls out hands in a long pipe crawls in Cass says sacred says Canunpa don't inhale, smoke is our prayers up to the spirit nation to sacred mystery Wakán Tanka hold with two hands with reverence like holding a baby careful careful I take Canunpa and shockwaves run through my chest my mother my father close inside I am scared of this power this sacred this Canunpa I want to hand it off quickly but Julian won't take it he motions to smoke smoke Canunpa

no thing between me and this sacred no priest no pastor no doctrine no safe camp away just me and this sacred in my hands me in the womb of Makáh nothing between

I smoke 'don't inhale' I hear again, billows of smoke rise move toward the center the tall pile of stone people in the center the watching compassionate ancient Inyan in the center Julian takes Canunpa and smokes then passes it again again it comes to me and sacred isn't so scary now I feel it - holding a beloved child to cherish to hold to love no words no words smoke again billows then it is done, tap your shoulders and pass it, Julian says then out the doorway to waiting Lee tenderness in his hands too they know this sacred have known all along time before and before back farther and farther these have found the way back

darkness again and sweet fragrance of cedar and sage healing smoke and tobacco smoke Canunpa clears my head my eyes see now in this darkness a deep purple orb lingers in the center where the stones lie - moves pulsates out to the edges then back to the center gathering strength first toward where Julian sits then to Lee then to Cass then to me a blinding flash of purple turning to white light then back to the center and now black and purple pulsate then around and around again moving with the song visible song I sing along learn it easy this time finding my way forward to find my way back

 Julian asks for Mni Olowan, the Water Song. Cass begins it in her clear haunting voice. Julian takes up the melody and Cass warbles and moves within and around it, like water flowing, moving over rocks as it travels downstream. Leaving and returning to the melody she creates the sound of water burbling.

I too join in this song breathing in the water, the healing of this sacred water.

The stone people too sing when Julian pours water on them. In my mind's eye I see the steam rising up from the stones then following a downward path along the curved sides of the Inipi until it reaches the cool earth and then moving toward the center flies up again from the heat of the stones. Falling and rising over and over while we alone are in stillness. My soul drinks in this Inipi, these customs this language like one who has wandered in the desert for years, lifetimes, without water. Jesus said he would give us living water to drink. Is this that water? This direct unfiltered unshielded relation to Jesus inside the holiest of holies? This is blasphemy to even think but dishonesty is impossible in here in the searing darkness.

Mitakuyas, mitakuyas and the door flap opens one last time. A cloud of steam pours out the door glowing white in the sunshine. Silence then Julian talking, Lee and Cass talking, no one wants to leave. I am at home in my silence no one says 'you're quiet tonight' no one presses a smile, a curtsey, a virtue, a person who never existed to replace the one who once did who once was who now is. I am at home here.

"I feel like a ghost in a good way," I say, finding my voice again, sifting the soft, cool earth through my fingers "New, but the same but new. I can't describe it. Like the air has cleared after a fog. Like, like . . . seeing different. I'm okay now."

"Wanagí," Julian says, "that's what you're feeling."

"Wanagí. Even this has a name."

"We have to take the Inipi down," Cass says. "I suspect things are falling apart back there," she says, motioning toward Zion with her chin.

"Can we go in one more time though? Tomorrow? I would go in every morning if I could. Start my day this way."

"We have to take it down," Julian says, looking at me sidewise.

Wade

❖

Out on the pasture the building crew gathers. With so many different projects I had no idea there were so many of us, all gathered together quietly in the sun, waiting for Paul. Some news and then back to work. These warm summer days it's harder to work than in the dreary winter months. The urge to hit the road and hitchhike cross country again wafts through like the welcome breezes only to be shut out by the demands of the day. It's focusing on the work keeps me going. Without the work I know I'd backslide for sure.

Finally not Paul but Jacob joins us asking for a circle so we are all able to hear and see each other, asks us to join hands as he prays, asking the Lord to be in our conversation.

"Liam is leaving the ministry. He's been caught in sin, caught in a series of lies and was planning to tour the houses this month with the intent to establish a kingdom unto himself alone, removing us and all other counsel, leaving himself as the only authority.

"We talked to him just moments ago, confronted him with

this and asked him to explain, give us his side of the story, to humble himself, seek counsel, repent. He refused it all so we told him we, as anointed elders, were removing him from his position as our pastor. He laughed in our faces and walked out. We're having this conversation now with everyone here in Zion, and all the houses and properties, the married couples - everyone in the ministry simultaneously. There is agreement among everyone we've spoken to so far that the only way the ministry can continue as a vessel of the Lord is if Liam leaves. There is no other option, no other way. His response left us no choice."

In the silence that follows Jacob lists all the other charges they aimed at Liam. A long list, I had no idea. See no evil, hear no evil, speak no evil.

Jacob looks at the circle of stunned faces, each of us unable to speak, each hoping someone else will say something. No one speaks, no one gets up and, more stunning, no one rejects this news. I don't reject the news, did I already know at some level?

"But how can God's anointed . . . ." Charlie's voice almost in a whisper trails off. Looking down he stands, turns away, to leave the group but then turns back and sits again. "He's God's anointed. He's the one whose visions from God never fail. He's the one who can hear the voice of the Lord most clearly. He's the one who walks into a room and the wind of the Holy Spirit blows through, blessing all the brethren waiting to hear his study."

"And this is what we've put our faith in," Jacob says, "the certainty that Liam was that man of God. We left off somewhere or were turned away at some point from our personal responsibilities in our walk."

"So what now?" Charlie asks.

"A Pastors' meeting will happen end of the month, two weeks from now. Nothing will change, really. Ours is a strong ministry, Samuel's been out visiting the Amish, been there the past three months sharing our ways, learning from them. He said we're very similar to them and we know how long their history is, how strong and enduring . . . ."

Liam hurries along the dirt road at the bottom of the pasture on his way to his trailer. He sees us and turns, walking up the pasture to join us, but Jacob stands up, full of authority, making his presence known. Liam stops, considers the group with Jacob standing between, a wall of defiance. Liam smiles cynically and walks off, shaking his head. A smile I recognize instantly.

"So it's done," I say.

"Yes. It's done."

Charlie

❖

It lasted five minutes, this meeting, and now Jacob is off to make phone calls to the houses around the country. The brothers all leave, back to their work, I assume. Wade and I stay out on the pasture, neither of us ready to get back to work. I lay back, watch the clouds drift by. Gradually a weight lifts. A weight I didn't know I was carrying and the odd sensation of freedom passes through me. Freedom from what I have no idea, the sensation floats on its own. So familiar and so long absent. The sheen of sin attaches to it and I whisper a repentance but my confession feels rote.

"I knew Marty didn't just take off, leave on his own, I fixed it in my mind to believe Liam, like I had to, but I knew it," I say, abruptly, finally speaking my thoughts. "I fixed it good so I didn't even think about it - until now. Fuck. Yes, fuck. Fuck me. I'm not staying. And you knew. You knew about Cass. We're a couple of cowards, I'd say."

"What? You knew what happened with Marty?"

"He told me when he was packing to go, that Liam had just

told him he was being moved to the men's house in town and then he remembered Liam said not to tell anyone. It was a set up. I'm leaving."

"Now? It'll be different now. Better. A better way to live in the Lord, you'll see."

"Not me," I say. "Not here. Hey, I'm relieved. I'm tired. And suddenly I'm not as hungry. Maybe all this gnawing hunger . . . never mind.

"I'm really ready to think for myself for a change. Feels like I've been tossed about in an unpredictable sea. Hanging onto a life raft like my life depended on it. The authority of Liam, the only thing to hang onto. Moving from one job to the next, moving from state to state, house to house. There's bound to be a church in town I can get involved in that won't demand my entire life."

"Who are you Charlie? Two hours ago you condemn me for questioning Liam's statement about Cass and Sawyer and now you're rejecting everything we've built here. How long you been thinking this way?"

"How about since now? Just now. I knew instantly when Jacob stood up and Liam walked away with that smirk on his face that it was over for me. It's of the Lord. It's. Of. The. Lord. That's what we always heard. Every move guided by the hand of God. But now I doubt it. Can't help but doubt it. I can't do this anymore. I'm done," I say, speaking to the clouds.

Wade stands, walks off, taking his tools. Back to work? The thought of going back to work saps the sudden jolt of energy this news gave me. Amazing the hold this ministry has had over me. The hold I gave it. Was it worth it? probably. But no more. A sucker. Have I been a sucker? Never mind, but no way I'm going back to work.

Instead I wander aimlessly, end up in the dining hall, the kitchen, an old habit. Dishes are on the tables but no one eating. No one has bothered to return their plates to the kitchen. Someone must have spoken to the brethren here while they ate. In the kitchen dough is rising but no one is here to punch it down, put it into loaf pans, bake it or serve it. How is it possible?

A mutiny, a simultaneous digression into what? Thinking for ourselves? After years of denial and acquiescence everyone vanished in this moment?

    I'm gonna take one last walk through the woods, that's what I'm gonna do. Get one last taste of nature before I head out, hitch hike out of here. On my way out I grab a few biscuits, slab on some butter, sneak a bit of honey but end up leaving it all behind. The desperation to be filled is gone.

Wade

❖

The tool shed is empty, Malcolm is gone, the door's wide open, and tools are scattered where the brothers just left them - on the floor, on the benches. I put my dirty shovel on the floor with some others. How long have I wanted to do that? Ha. Outside I hear voices coming from the dorm. Giddy voices, nervous hushed voices talking about where and how they'll get on with their lives voices. Brothers are hurriedly packing the few things they own. Most have an extra pair of jeans or a second shirt or pair of shoes, some have amassed more. It feels like simultaneous relief and exhaustion taking over. Each looking to their own uncertain future with a mixture of excitement and fear. So different. Sentiments long since considered the height of sin.

And what about the horses? Lily's gone and Liam's on his way out and if we all leave they'll have no one to care for them. I throw down some hay, fill up the water barrels to the tops and imagine opening the barn doors so they can find their way in the wild. Better than starving out here. But maybe I'll stay behind, take care of the horses, live in Liam's trailer. Maybe I'll do that.

Paul

❖

The woods are fragrant with the smell of honey and wild berries. Bending down I gather a cluster of blackberries from a low branch among the brambles and vines. Sweet and tart both, these young berries are still clawing their way to sunlight and ripeness and some are not ready to eat so I pick carefully. "What happens to fruit when it's not ready to harvest?" I remember someone asking me one night when I was out evangelizing, trying to force a conversion. "It resists," he said. "And if picked before it's ready it rots. And if eaten it strikes the tongue with bitterness - the taste of one convinced, coerced, persuaded." Even now these phone calls, the urgent calls convincing the married couples in town to reject Liam based on our word. Our word. It felt right among the elders, after the tenth call it felt like coercion.

I gather up handfuls of the ripest berries and hold them to my nose, try to hold off a slowly building panic that it's over. This place, this way of life, my hard earned position as an elder. Who am I if I'm not an elder with prestige and authority?

My old life looms hard against these years of importance. If not this life then maybe the military or some church in town. A place I can again attain to a position. A position. Is that what this has been? No, I don't believe it.

The trail has changed since I first came, since the logging. Money for the ministry, Liam said and for the health of the forest. But it's different, the forest is no longer a forest, more like a thicket with trees scattered. The smell of smoke drifts from the other side of our creek. I follow the trail and the smoke smell onto BLM territory where the trees haven't been logged, where sunlight filters through more dappled, and end up at a small opening where the sun filters through in a shaft. There, inside a crescent of stones is a fire pit with red coals opposite a small domelike structure covered with blankets. Between the pit and the dome is a mound of dirt with a staff and feathers a long pipe and someone's earrings, a couple packets of Bugler tobacco - and Charlie, Charlie! sitting on a log.

Charlie shushes me when I begin to ask what's going on here, shrugs his shoulders, motions for me to join him, and mocks a cynical laugh but seems transfixed, silently listening to a drum and the singing from inside the dome.

Shutting off the raging in my head is easy here, listening to the sound of the drum - like the sound of a heartbeat. I sit on the ground and lean against the log beside my brothers, drink in the stillness of this small circle of light, close my eyes, instantly relax.

When the singing stops a flap opens and a dense cloud of steam escapes, drifts upward and diffuses into the firs. Then voices from inside. Cass's voice and Lily's, Cass who I've judged so harshly. Finally Julian, the Indian man who tracked with Lily, crawls out followed by Cass, Lily and another man who also looks Indian. They see us but say nothing, they shake hands with each other as they emerge from the little dome, forming a line and then each finds a comfortable place to sit except for Lily who comes over to greet us. With no explanation she shakes our hands. "Welcome," she says. Just that. Then she turns away and sits in a sunny spot, leaning against the dome with eyes closed. Her face relaxed. For the first time since I've known her she seems at peace, truly and actually at peace. Something about this humble welcome from Lily outside the tenants of the ministry, is threatening everything I've armed myself against.

Watching Lily, just sitting there relaxed, brings on a wave of vertigo as I realize I now will have to face who I really am without the protection of the ministry, the protection of righteousness that I wear like a mask, or more like armor. Believing myself armed against the moment that changed my life, the moment I couldn't undo. So I turned to the Lord to make it go away but it didn't go away; It just went underground and festered. The look on Jesse's face when I stabbed him in that dark, filthy alley, in my drunken rage. My hand reaching up to feel the sticky blood and the gash he left on my face. The scar Liam called proof of God's goodness to forgive, God's power to wash away my sin. And in my desperation I believed it was a cause for rejoicing, believing in the goodness of God and that I was forgiven - my sin truly washed away. How is that even possible? Jesse is still dead and that will never go away.

It feels wrong to talk. I don't know why but Charlie and I just sit and watch, like intruders or voyeurs. I want to stay and go at the same time. "What is this?" I say, finally.

"It's n'dn way," Cass says. "This is called Inipi, Inipi ceremony for purification. We were hoping no one would come upon it."

Lily smiles in our direction. Something different, no deference? the submissive posture gone? Purification ceremony hmm. Somehow Lily makes this less threatening. Lily calm and at peace after Andrew, after all that madness. If Lily can . . . .

"The ministry is breaking apart. It's over," I say. "Jacob told us Liam lied about you Cass. And Sawyer. And Marty. He kicked Marty out to silence him? and . . . everyone is dispersing, gathering their things and just walking off. Feels like the rapture in reverse." Lily and Cass just listen without comment or surprise.

"We, the elders, asked Liam to leave. We asked him to repent or leave the ministry. He didn't repent. It just happened. Just now. There was a meeting with Jacob, with the other elders, they told us how he had been planning to remove all authority but his own. A kingdom unto himself, is how Jacob put it." I'm babbling but now I've started I can't stop. "Then I made phone calls to the married couples, and someone talked to you guys?" I ask Charlie. "It just happened just now. He didn't repent."

For a long time everyone sits quietly, rests peacefully. No one speaks and no one stirs. A quiet after the storm. Then Julian gets up and starts taking down the blankets. The other Indian man joins him, carefully folding blankets, making a neat pile. Cass instructs Lily and in silence they take scissors and cut and remove the colored cloth that holds the inner structure of branches together while Julian and the other man stand watch. The cloth goes on a small blanket set aside. There are also strings of small colored bundles that hang from the inner branches on lengths of yarn, these too are gathered and placed on the blanket. Once this is done Lily and Cass take handfuls of the cloth and the bundles and place them with care onto the red embers.

Smoke billows up, the smell of tobacco fills the air. Watching the smoke billow up, breathing in the smoke, the smell of tobacco, my body begins to relax. There is a feeling of deep respect for each movement, for each moment, for each thing handled even to the small bit of yarn that fell off to the side - of every action having meaning. The quiet and the foreignness of it are peaceful against the backdrop of the last half hour and the stark reality of seeing clearly for the first time what's behind me, and the uneasy reality of not knowing what's ahead.

Lily leaves the others and sits beside us after putting the last bits of cloth on the embers. The men begin to move the branches into a pile. I stand up to help but Lily motions no and for me to sit down. From our log we watch the men move the branches into a pile. Without the cloth holding them together, the branches that made up the dome shape of the structure slip down to the ground, the ones set into the earth are pulled up and carefully placed together. Still no one speaks.

Lily leaves us and with Cass takes the thin branches by small armfuls and carefully places them in the fire, gently as if caring for something - these branches - with deep meaning and connection. Again the men keep watch. Flames rise high in the forest, the nearest trees seem far enough to escape the sparks but I wonder if this fire is consuming more than the structure here in the woods. I wonder that our whole ministry is going up in flames simultaneously on the other side of the creek.

Again Lily sits beside us and together we all watch the fire. Cass and the men come over to where Lily, Charlie, and I are sitting, Lily stands and we stand. It all feels so foreign but at the same time natural. Some buried instinct? Julian shakes my hand, thanks me for being there, for being a witness to this ceremony, says I'm welcome to stay while they finish up, then shakes Charlie's hand. The other Indian man says his name is Lee, shakes my hand.

When Cass shakes my hand, the reality of it all hits in a moment - the loss of our community and way of life, the unfair treatment toward Cass we've all been a part of all these years, my part in it all. Tears threaten to come and I can't make eye contact anymore but Cass is not fooled and she leans in and hugs me. The compassion I feel is overwhelming after the years of hardness, learned hardness, and superiority toward the sisters. Lily follows Cass and shakes our hands last simply saying thank you. Then we all sit and watch in silence as the fire burns down to coals.

"What about the horses?" Julian asks.

Cass says they're her horses. That Liam gave them to her as a peace offering just before Lily came back to Zion. "I would love to take them," she says. "But I have no way to keep them. I can barely keep myself."

"My ceremony is a couple of moons away, early August," Julian says. "If you can't find another place for them I could take them, to present them to my elders in South Dakota for you. Their homestead ranges through grassland and forests, the horses would be well cared for and loved."

"You could ride them all the way," Lee says. "You and Lily just take off and go. N'dn way, ayee," Cass and Julian smile, nod.

"I would be honored if you would make that prayer for us and present the horses in a good way." Cass says.

PART IV

Lily

❖

My father and I gaze out at the late afternoon waves, mesmerized by the beauty as the sun lowers to the horizon. Nothing between us and the blue expanse of ocean, of sky, of whitecaps and gulls. The blue and the white. Listen to crash of waves. The only sound but for the gulls.

"Do you still believe?" He asks.

Stillness grips as I look inward, feel through the months of change and awareness that brought me this far. Brought me to such a great distance that I no longer feel any connection to the ministry or the life that held me for those four years. Yet one last thread holds and my father's question brings it to the surface, the final thread keeping me. That old familiar tug of condemnation? a knee jerk reaction now that I've come this far? Recognizing my calcified faith, calcified religion, calcified, calcified. Idolatry in the fashion of a golden calf, my cross to bear? or, or of Jesus who stands at the door and knocks. You did let him in. So deal with it.

Have I not left at all? This moment of hesitation, of

condemnation, says no. I know in this moment I'm still held to this believing through fear. The last thread is fear. Not faith. Not not Jesus, not even lingering doubt - just fear. Hell that was always present is what holds me in this moment but without faith Hell has no power, it can not stand.

Like stepping over a threshold I answer, "no."

One word. That is all. Just that. And the bond is broken.

I walk from the house down the little trail and across Highway 1 just as the sun is dipping below the horizon, down the thousand steps to the little cove just south of the pier. Bare feet stepping onto sand. Grain upon grain the sand moves and shifts yielding to my weight, the earth receiving my presence, the sand moving lifelike. Sharp pungency of salt spray the touch of mist on skin fearsome waves crashing at right angles

a bowl

a cauldron

a place of becoming or extinguishing.

Cool crisp shock of water takes my breath away as I plunge deep in this dance this game. LaMer, the song in my head since I ran from the land of Zion, sings clear. I float through a silky buoyant sea. One that had been my childhood friend but never before experienced this way. How possible? I grew up here. How possible I'd never known the silksea, never smelled her fragrance or tasted her salt like this before? Like being born again, this time into my own body, my own immediate experience - say the word and you will be born again - I laugh at the irony of it.

The disappearing sun casts the sky now a steely gray, the sea reflects back the dimming change. The full moon rises in the east, a mirror image of the setting. Looking east at her giant orb the first of the big waves catches me off guard. Tumbling underwater, the grind of sand, the violence, shocks to attention. Coming up for air the next waves come from three sides shaping a bowl, my small body deep in the sinking cauldron. Shock of fear rises but I know to run, to swim, toward the onslaught of water, the walls of water, and into the waves, to run toward my fears, the ocean my teacher the one I forgot in the cowering. The third waves come bigger than the first two but this time I am ready. Swimming hard toward the wave I fly over the crest and the stinging spray to the calm beyond.

In the lull between sets I drift, floating easily on my back, bobbing yet watchful in the graceful arms of LeMer. The pull of the tide seduces, its primal voice calling enticing to lull, to float, to allow, to go out to sea. In this peace, looking back, I try to remember who I was. And I cannot. Try to remember the one who was innocent, naïve, the person who was. The one before putting on the cloak of perfection in case He comes in just that moment and I am judged. Is it even possible? Is she gone for good?

Lee said write back from the before time and find her. Spin a tale, write a history or a fantasy or write nonsense but don't self censor. She'll reemerge you'll be surprised. "Stay with the heat," a wise man once said. Such easy guidance. Find your way back and move forward from there. Peel away the shoulds the identities the the . . . .

Surfers float further out, waiting for the perfect wave. "You're in a rip tide," I hear, "swim to the side."

I wave, call out a thank you and swim out of the pull. Swim to the side. Step aside. The earth my teacher.

Dry land seems a long distance and between here and there the waves crash most violently. Timing is everything. I wait for the next set and after the big waves pass I carefully work my way out of the water.

Just beyond reach of the waves and wet sand a small fire glows. Around it a circle of women. "Join," I hear. I watch it move to open, snakelike it opens its mouth and I join. They speak in soft voices as they pass around a bitter medicine. "Drink," they say and I drink.

Just above whisper voices tell stories of a people of long ago who were led by the women. The woman nation they said, woman nation, something familiar about these words sends a shiver through my chest. Julian speaking of the woman nation, the stone nation . . . .

So many fires I've known. This one has its own meaning. Fire of release, fire of returning, fire of reclaiming myself - whatever that ends up being. The women sing softly then they too drum, again this familiarity.

Solitude's dreaming dances before my eyes: An image embodied in women just like these, around a fire just like this, smoke swirled and gazing just like this. Singing, all as one, one as all, they rise and take off their clothes while I, sitting, watch and wonder. Long hair streaming in the moonlight, glittering in firelight, the hair of Medusa yet I am not stone turned. I move now among them, slow then dancing. Laughing they drum. Beating sticks against skins stretched over embroidery hoops. Hoops in revolt, women in revolt.

Beneath the foamwaves fisheyes watch. The earth alive beneath the sand. Beneath my toes the movement of time released from its boundaries while all around me women drum for their lives. Then She appears and one by one we turn to face her. She, now within the circle absorbing light and sound, releases it back into the wind charged with the visions of our dreaming.

Dancing in deathrags She sings the rhythms of blood and fire cleaving to the earth until rocks rise up in the East - protectors, vast protectors of the night - lending their shadowy wills to our desires. They rise higher and higher until the dawn and the day and the warming when they will with one last effort hold off the sun. But for now we dance, She among us speaking in other tongues, singing the rhythms of the night.

"Come, join us, we travel together our van is just down the coast from here. We work together and sing to the Goddess."

But I know now the scaffolding only holds up for so long then it becomes a straitjacket. These visions of the night, the life giving waves, and the stillborn invitation blend together in beauty. But I say no. No to these that I might say yes to the unknown, to running toward my fears.

What I long for is the resonance of darkness and sweat and of searing heat. Heat to the skinsides that heals and does not silence. Heat that gives rise to singing, and memory, and walking the earth. Walking beyond city and town, down into the desert and the forest bottom and across the across. Maybe someday meet up with Julian? So familiar, this way of being, yet so distant. So deep in the soul. Soul that gives courage to go forward. This is what I want, a tightrope walk to fall or to balance, not theirs to offer a net below. I retrieve my towel and make my way up the thousand steps to the highway.

❖

THE POSSESSED

A NOTE ABOUT THE AUTHOR

Susan Walcott has received the Raymond Fabrizio Memorial Humanities Division Book Grant Award for Excellence in Writing and the highest UDWPE Award for Excellence in Writing from the University of Arizona.

She lives in co-housing in Tucson, Arizona.